THE LIFE AND MIRACLES OF
ST IVO

by

S. B. Edgington

THE FRIENDS OF THE NORRIS MUSEUM

First published 1985

ISBN 0 9507209 4 1

Friends of the Norris Museum
Norris Library and Museum
The Broadway
St Ives, Cambridgeshire PE17 4BX

Printed and bound in Great Britain by Galliard (Printers) Ltd, Great Yarmouth

CONTENTS

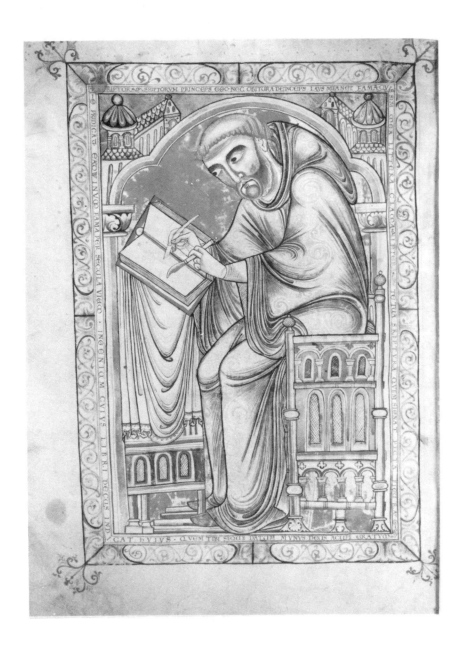

The Illustrations

All the drawings used to illustrate this book are the work of a twelfth century Canterbury monk. They were not drawn for St Ivo — none of the surviving manuscripts is illustrated — but for a psalter, or book of psalms. The artist was copying from an earlier psalter, now in Utrecht, and his pictures represent in a lively way the dress and occupations of the sort of people involved in St Ivo's story.

I thank the Master and Fellows of Trinity College, Cambridge for permission to reproduce the drawings from the Canterbury Psalter (MS R.17.1).

Acknowledgements

I am grateful to the following institutions who have allowed me access to manuscripts: the British Library manuscripts department; the Bodleian Library, Oxford; Trinity College, Dublin; Douai Town Library (for microfilm).

I should also like to thank the staff of Cambridge University Library, Huntingdon County Library, Huntingdon County Record Office, the Norris Library and Huntingdon Technical College Library who have assisted my research in many ways.

Finally I wish to put on record my gratitude to my colleagues at Huntingdon Technical College: not only to Geoff Pawling, who has read the script at various stages, and Veda Collingwood who enabled me to process all these words, but also to the rest, who may not be aware how greatly I value their friendship and support.

1 SLEPE

Slepe in the year 1000 was an unremarkable fen-edge village. It was sited at a river-crossing, but judging by its name (which means 'muddy'), it offered no clear advantage over Hemingford upstream or Holywell downstream as a crossing place. The most significant thing about late tenth-century Slepe was that the entire parish was part of the estates of Ramsey Abbey.

The Abbey was one of several, including Thorney, Crowland, Peterborough and Ely, which had been founded or refounded towards the end of the tenth century. They all followed the Benedictine Rule and looked upon the fenland countryside as perhaps equally a penance and a challenge. There is no reason to think that the tenth century landscape was any different from the eighth century as described by Felix:

> There is in the midland region of England a fearful marsh of immense size which, beginning from the Granta river not far from Grantchester, extends from the south to the North Sea in a long marshy waste, now with pools, now swampy, here and there with black vaporous streams, also with wooded island outcroppings and winding river-courses.

or indeed the eighteenth as described by Defoe:

> ...these Fens appeared overwhelmed by water...also covered by fogs, so that when the Downs and higher grounds of the adjacent country glistered with the beams of the sun, the Isle of Ely seemed wrapped up in mist and darkness, so that nothing could be discovered but now and then the Cupola of Ely Minster.

Given the drawbacks of their environment, it is not surprising if the abbeys were eager to seize any opportunity to improve their living or increase their wealth. They all built up estates in and beyond the fens, but while the other abbeys drew their endowments from a variety of sources, Ramsey's acquisitions were a special case.

Ramsey Abbey was founded in 969 by a layman, Ailwyn the ealdorman, and a churchman, Oswald, archbishop of York. In choosing to situate his new abbey in this part of the world St Oswald was probably influenced by family considerations. He was related to the wife of one Aethelstan Mannessone (son of Mann), a local landowner and she

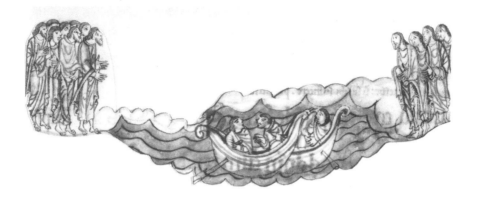

in turn was mother of Eadnoth who was at that time a monk at Worcester. Eadnoth was brought by Oswald to the new house at Ramsey and became its first abbot on Oswald's death in 992.

Abbot Eadnoth was keen to increase Ramsey's estates and during his abbacy Ramsey received large donations of land from a few families, in contrast with the way in which the other four fenland abbeys attracted many smaller and more scattered endowments. A special situation thus arose whereby Ramsey's benefactors took a close interest in the abbey's affairs, and in turn the abbey took every opportunity to recognize their generosity.

Thus it was with the Mannessone family. Aethelstan died in 986 having made a will. One provision was that his land in Slepe should go to his youngest daughter Alfwenna, with reversion to Ramsey if she died without heirs. There followed a complicated three-sided dispute in which one of the parties was Ramsey Abbey and another a priest called Osward who was a relation of Alfwenna. It was finally resolved and Ramsey Abbey gained outright ten hides of land at Slepe. This block of land with ten hides adjoining at Woodhurst and Old Hurst formed the largest holding of Ramsey Abbey at that time and at Domesday (1086).

A tract of land at Chatteris enabled Eadnoth to set up a nunnery there and he installed his sister Alfwenna, that same youngest daughter of Aethelstan Mannessone, as its first prioress. In this case he seemingly saw a need, since the nearest nunnery at the time was at Barking in Essex, and at the same time a chance to express the Abbey's appreciation to a major benefactor.

There is no reason to doubt that he hoped in the same way to develop a priory cell at Slepe and was on the look-out for a suitable opportunity or excuse to do so. Already in 1000 there was a monk who acted as bailiff or reeve (*praepositus*). He was another Eadnoth and grandson to Earl Alfwold the brother of Ailwyn the ealdorman, also archbishop Oswald's nephew, according to Goscelin — all of which illustrates the strength of family ties at the time. He was assisted by a steward (*vilicus*) who in 1001 was also the village smith.

The year 1000 was not chosen at random to start this study. It was a very significant date throughout Christendom, for it had been widely believed that the millennium would witness Christ's second coming; the end of the temporal world. The approach and passing of the date seem to have left people prey to all sorts of spiritual influences, and while the tenth century was the period of the monastic reform movement which included Ramsey's foundation, the eleventh saw the inspiration of the crusades, and marked the height of the cult of relics.

This mediaeval obsession with physical remains and reminders of Christ and his saints is difficult to comprehend today, although modern adulation of sporting and entertainment figures offers some comparisons. In those days life was less secure and belief in an omnipotent God more widespread. People felt a need for intermediaries in their dealings with the Almighty and this led to the veneration of saints, who were more approachable by ordinary people and might be relied upon to intercede for them with God. Relics were believed to focus the power of the saint in a particular place and enabled worshippers to identify with a patron or protector. The possession of such relics was a draw to pilgrims.

Relics could be whole skeletons, as in the case of St Ivo and his companions, or fragments such as teeth, hair, tears, milk or nail-clippings. They could be articles of clothing, splinters of the True Cross or more bizarre objects which had at some time belonged to or touched Christ and his saints. Needless to say fakes and forgeries were in abundance but even this did not really matter since the importance of relics was the focusing power they lent to people's belief, a sort of hot-line through a saintly exchange to the Almighty.

The way in which relics were obtained also did not affect their efficacy. They were commonly stolen; not only looted from the infidels in Palestine or the heretics in Byzantium, but also taken by theft from other Christian churches. This was how the monastery at Eynesbury had obtained the bones of St Neot from Cornwall in the late 900s. What is indisputable is that a new foundation like Ramsey needed relics almost as much as it needed land. Relics brought with them the patronage of a saint, prestige in the competition with other monasteries, and, most of all, popular devotion, both from the local people and from pilgrims.

It was the cult of relics that affected Slepe: for 1000 was also the last year of its obscurity. The story of Slepe's awakening can be read as it was recorded later in the eleventh century:

> A villager struggling to furrow the earth with a plough hit against a holy coffin. Astonished and excited by the hope of wealth, he called back the oxen, which were at a standstill, and put every effort into clearing the site. And when he realised that it was a human burial he called his fellow ploughmen to him. When the cover was lifted they found religious tokens suggesting a priest. They were captivated by the shining brightness of a chalice there; thinking it silver they vied with each other to break it in pieces. They seized the priestly brooches, transparent with the lustre of glass, which Ramsey Abbey afterwards inherited with the holy body and those same fragments of the chalice.

> A monk arrived swiftly, bailiff of the village, with the smith who was steward. Then abbot Eadnoth nearby was quickly fetched by a messenger, and after the remains of the man who was so clearly God's servant had been carefully washed he had them carried into the church and placed next to the altar. The common people, hurrying there with their spirits raised,

wished that the Lord, who had permitted this thing to be found, would also permit its identity to be known.

Therefore, so that it would be obvious that the discovery had been made not by a lucky chance but by God's will, glorious Ivo appeared the following night to the smith of that same village as he slept. He was a harmless and simple man—to such the Lord speaks face to face, and entrusts his secrets, and he reveals to children things hidden from the wise.

The saint was tall in stature; he had a white face, a lifelike appearance and a burning gaze; he had with him a priestly fillet and crozier, and he held out an archbishop's cross. He soothed the man, who was astonished by the vision, with an unusually sweet voice, and said: "The body you are surprised to have found just now in such a place is mine: I am bishop Ivo, who was buried here and have lain hidden with my blessed companions until now. Go tomorrow and measure out the place eight feet on the right-hand side of my grave, and you will find the tomb of one of my holy companions. The other also who was buried with us is to be found not far away, and these two exult with me in glory. When you are convinced by these proofs, supply them to the bailiff from me so that he will tell abbot Eadnoth who may translate me with these my companions to the community at Ramsey."

Truly, since the poor man was terrified in spirit to report these heavenly orders, on the following night his negligence was rebuked and he was reproached by the same power. None the less on the third night while he was still hesitating, when he was in his first sleep the teacher himself appeared; and now he charged him quite severely with disobedience, and as the smith trembled and demanded a sign, he struck him with his bishop's crozier: "And you will have this sign," he said, "and will never get rid of it, unless you tell what you have been ordered to."

Waking up after this the smith was sore in the place where he had felt the blow, as if he had been stabbed with a sword. And when he had reported the orders along with his painful sign, the man himself recovered: however the bailiff refused to believe the saint's great revelation, and pushed away the villager as if he was relating some fantastic tale. "And should we translate," he said, "and glorify the worthless remains of some old cobbler as those of a saint?"

His nightly sleep overcame the scoffer, and the holy bishop, seeming rather severe in manner and appearance, woke him up with a harsh speech: "Get up," he said, "get up as quickly as possible. For I am that man whom yesterday you mocked as a cobbler and I have made for you leggings that will last. Put them on, and you will ride home in them in memory of me." At these words the sleeping man stood up and sat down again: his just reprover had fashioned leggings very tightly for his legs. And so, struck down like this, he woke up, and then a very severe pain tied up all his shinbones from the feet up and he could neither stand nor walk. He rode to the monastery on someone else's horse; and after he entered he reported all his own pains one by one, which he had refused to believe when they happened to someone else: and with much sorrow as well as in a truthful voice he proclaimed those things which he had condemned as fantasies.

Needless to say the abbot Eadnoth was 'delighted at such a wealth of unexpected treasure' and he himself hurried to Slepe and seized a spade to uncover Ivo's companions. In the general rejoicing it was noted that the discovery was made on 24th April 1001, in Ethelred's reign, and exactly ten years after Ailwyn the founder's death (which, however, was in 992, a discrepancy which cannot be reconciled).

In case you feel that the poor bailiff Eadnoth was treated with inordinate harshness for his (not unreasonable) doubts, you may find comfort as the writer of the *Miracles* does in the fact that he made a good death, though for the last fifteen years of his life he was crippled. St Ivo appeared to him a week before he died and said:

"The time is now at hand when the lashes with which I seized you may become a healthy cure for you; and, having lived for a long time in darkness, you may have the most welcome day of eternal happiness: for on the seventh day from now, just be ready—I shall come to take you up from this prison of flesh into our light."

So the bailiff had endured his purgatory in life and could go straight to heaven.

St Ivo's mortal remains had meanwhile been translated to Ramsey with great ceremony and watched by a huge crowd:

they flocked here from countryside and town: the open fields could scarcely hold the rush of people. Prayers and hymns of praise graced the air: heaven itself seemed to favour the saints, the sun seemed to rejoice with all its rays, such a sweet season and clear day had dawned.

2 WHO WAS ST IVO?

It will be clear already from the story of the saint's discovery that he had a very nasty way with people who doubted him — and there are many other examples.

One explanation for his sensitivity comes at once to mind: everything known about the saint came from himself; there was no corroborative evidence. Even his name and the fact that he was an archbishop were supplied by Ivo in a dream. Our information comes ultimately from a single source, the *Life and Miracles of St Ivo* by Goscelin.

This Goscelin wrote towards the end of the eleventh century. He claimed to be abridging a *Life* written by abbot Andrew Withman (Leucander) who had travelled to Jerusalem in 1020 and on his return put down all he knew of Ivo, who was famous in Greece. Withman's account does not survive but Goscelin is considered a reliable and conscientious historian, and it is unlikely the earlier writing was a fabrication of his. The story is thus:

> The apostolic teacher, and messenger of the true sun, glorious bishop Ivo, rose in Persia, like the morning star, destined by the Lord for the western lands of Britain. He left his sweet homeland as an exile, fellow citizen of heavenly powers, and as Christ's pilgrim he went through the world looking for the eternal kingdom. Wherever he arrived he shone brightly with his rays; scattering words he filled everything with Christ's gospel; he brought peoples and nations to the Saviour by his lessons and examples and countless miracles.
>
> After Great Asia, after Illyricum, after Rome, after traversing countless cities and peoples, he entered Gaul, and there he sparkled none the less with such signs that wonderful powers proclaimed his heavenly life and angelic teaching. And when the king of the Franks and the nobility of the kingdom and the people tried to keep him there — such an angel of God was he — with fitting honours, he, who had fled as an exile from the worldly glory of his parents and was fighting his way through many trials to enter the kingdom of God, could not be kept back by any earthly favour.
>
> Therefore, with all his acts confirmed by faith, he crossed the sea with his worthy comrades and companions to white Albion of Britain; and according as the Lord granted, he took pity on the white peoples with fatherly devotion and, as much by miracles as by preaching, he released them from the error of idolatry and more truly purified them with baptism. There was also, following the very loving father, a young man of

noble rank called Patricius, son of a certain senator, who for the love of Christ, calling him through St Ivo, not only disregarded his gentle birth and hereditary honours, but truly even deserted the maiden betrothed to him and with her all hope of descendants, and stuck inseparably to his gentle master as much out of affection as from imitation. Blessed is he who followed the example of John, that most intimate and bosom friend of Christ.

Then the healthgiving foreigner Ivo proceeded into the province of Mercia, to the town which is named Huntingdon, and to the next village which is called Slepe. Because he knew he had been led by the Lord to this particular place he persisted there for many years to the end of his life. Here indeed he assumed his divine role with such ardour, as if only now at last he had begun, and as if after a long thirst he had found the spring he sought. Here, I say, by keeping watch perpetually for his own life as well as everyone else's; here by waiting for the Lord right to the end, his lamps of virtue blazing with an aura of chastity, at last he opened up with joy to the one who came and knocked; and the Lord's Ivo went to the Lord, who had left the Father and come into the world, and from the conquered world brought back the victory of the chosen people. Here his home was made in peace, and in peace he was buried: where, although he lay hidden from men's knowledge for about four hundred years (as is calculated from the discovery which follows), his name lives for ever.

It must be said that the story is fraught with improbabilities. It is not utterly impossible. Under the Sassanid dynasty in Persia the Nestorian Christians were celebrated for their missionary activity—admittedly more so in the Far East than Europe. (It is notable that there was a bishop Iso-Yahb I of Arzun (582-595) who sounds a bit like Ivo of Asitania and who had to leave his see, but his death among the Arabs is documented and there seems to be no other possible candidate.) However, if the date 600 is accurate Ivo would have arrived in England ahead of Augustine and settled in Mercia some seventy years before its conversion as recorded by Bede. In this case it has to be said that Ivo was not a very effective missionary! The sheer unlikeliness of the story is the only thing that argues for a grain of truth. Why invent a Persian saint?

We cannot discount the possibility of a kernel of local tradition or folk memory. The story could be an indication of Celtic survival in the area, with its memory of the oriental origins of Christianity. The *Life of St Guthlac* has been interpreted as indicating large-scale survival of 'Ancient Britons' in the fens. Furthermore one of Ivo's companions was named Patrick (Patricius), a name, like Ivo, more Celtic than Persian sounding.

Goscelin reinforces this possibility in a chapter about prophecies:

> Another thing seems to concern an ancient reference to our patron: at the village which is named Hirst there is a field called Ivo's. Also before these times there was a very old man in Rome, talking to someone who came from England to pray, and when he learnt he was English he questioned him rather closely as to whether he knew a village called Slepe. When the stranger replied that he knew it very well the old man continued with these words: "Believe this, and preserve it as my memory begins to fail: not far from the ford in the nearby river some very bright light-bringers lie hidden who in their own time will be raised up and clearly known." The Englishman returned to his own country and with joyous faith spread the news of these things which afterwards were revealed to us and which today the truth has proved. A certain faithful priest, Durandus by name, also survived to these times, and he quite often promised those things which we have seen done.

A suggestion both ingenious and simple has been made: if the stone coffin was, as seems likely, a Roman burial, parts of an inscription may have been decipherable — perhaps IVO and the Roman name PERSIUS? There is, of course, no evidence now to support this attractive hypothesis.

Goscelin's *Life* of the saint is really not a biography at all. He described the growth of a cult. This has to be viewed in the context of eleventh century Huntingdonshire.

The time is important: this was the great age of relics as has been explained. Monastic houses were prepared to go to amazing lengths to acquire relics, especially new foundations who were seeking prestige. In Ramsey's case this desire for relics was heightened by the local competition, the nearest being Eynesbury which, although Benedictine, looked to Bec in Normandy. The monks of Eynesbury had conducted a daring bone-raid in Cornwall and carried off the skeleton of St Neot in the late tenth century. So far Ramsey had acquired the bones of two young Kentish princes murdered in 664 and a fragment of the True Cross given by Aethelstan Mannessone, but something more local and exclusive would add greatly to its attractions. For relics had more than a spiritual value; they were also great 'crowd-pullers', attracting the pilgrims who were the nucleus of the tourist trade of the age.

What is interesting and unusual is that Ramsey's relics of St Ivo were found rather than looted, stolen and/or bequeathed. If they were not the bones of a Persian bishop, then their speedy acclamation as such suggests a triumph of opportunism on the part of abbot Eadnoth of Ramsey. It would be alien to the eleventh century mind to interpret it as cynical exploitation; rather the discovery was surely seen, quite literally, as a Godsend. The abbot quelled any doubts he might have had, accepting the chance he was looking for to establish a religious centre on the Mannessone lands and seeing perhaps already how Slepe could be developed as a market-centre once the tourist-pilgrims had beaten a path to the shrine. The same process, after all, was already under way at Eynesbury/St Neots.

The germ of St Ivo's tale may well have been a local folk memory. Anyway its vagueness offered certain advantages, and elaborations began early. The *Lives* of saints were read (for instance) at monastic mealtimes, and edifying passages were more easily swallowed if spiced with circumstantial detail and sensational episodes. Other *Lives* from the same era show a similar taste for the exotic.

Moreover the saint's dubious identity meant that his story could be developed to suit the political climate. Thus in the 1090s when Goscelin wrote his version, it may have been a positive advantage not to be Anglo-Saxon, and Ivo's oriental origins were stressed. Ivo also gained royal parentage which allowed him to compete with the Anglo-Saxon royal saints. Ivo's parents are entirely fictitious but they illustrate the soap-opera elements which the mediaeval audience enjoyed.

> In the city Frianeos, where they say St Ivo and his brother Athanatus were born, their father, whose name was Yomos, reigned, and their mother Ysitalia was queen. Moreover Athanatus lived the life of a hermit in a certain wood: through his merits this lord has been been thought worthy to work many miracles.
>
> St Ivo also was born in this city and as he deserved became bishop; and not long afterwards he was appointed to an archbishopric in the city of Asitania, and he stayed on, watchful over the flock entrusted to him, obeying God devoutly: until because of the people's sins a famine grew so great that mother ate daughter, and father son, and many prelates ate the people in their charge. As a result twelve religious men left their own land and chose to travel through many regions as a pilgrimage. When they had arrived in Rome they separated from one another on the pope's advice, and St Ivo, as appointed by God, entered Britain with his nephew Sithius and his relation Iuthius and some other people.
>
> St Athanatus indeed returned to the wilderness where he had lived before and ended his life; his body remains there

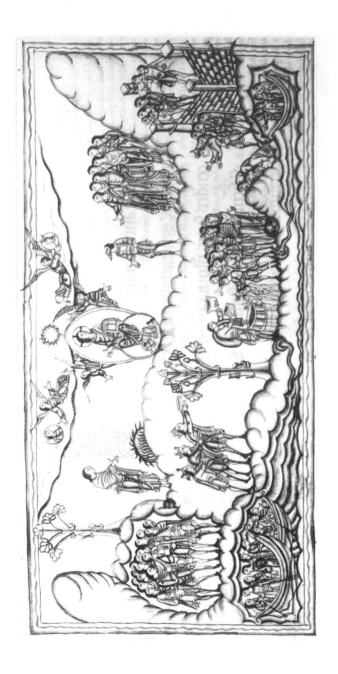

uncorrupted to this day on a certain high mountain. He is honoured by a community of monks, and every single month his fingernails are cut, his hair is trimmed, and he is honoured and cherished by everyone throughout the whole region of Greece.

Such persiflage does not help us to arrive at St Ivo's identity. Since the bones and the 'religious tokens' found with them disappeared at the time of the Dissolution in 1539 we cannot positively say whether they were indeed relics of an Anglo-Saxon bishop, as the pontificals suggest, or whether they were Roman remains (pagan or Christian) interpreted with the eye of faith and hope. Archaeology has discovered Roman layers on the site of the later priory but this is far from conclusive evidence: for one thing there may be few settlement sites close to fords where Roman remains would not be found in this area; for another, you would not normally expect to find domestic remains in the near vicinity of a formal burial, since one of the strongest taboos in Roman times led to cemeteries being outside town and village boundaries.

In the end it is just not possible to tell what the monks of Ramsey found in 1001. And in the end it probably hardly matters since the growth of the cult of St Ivo did not depend on his 'reality'. He was what we might now call a media creation, the central figure in an advertising campaign which eventually brought considerable wealth and prosperity to the abbey of Ramsey and the village of Slepe.

Abbot Eadnoth had probably only the first glimmerings of the possibilities of Slepe in 1001. He was made bishop of Dorchester in 1006 and died ten years later fighting for Edmund Ironside at the battle of Assendun. The victor in that battle, the Danish king Cnut, gave his royal favour to Ramsey but did nothing for the priory cells, perhaps because they were Eadnoth's project. Nevertheless the cell at Slepe survived through the eleventh century and was visited by pilgrims from near and far, as the miracles show. The market and fair in Slepe probably also had their origins in this period: the charter of 1110 whereby Henry I granted a fair to 'St Benedict of Ramsey and St Ivo of Slepe' was not for the usual 'vigil, feast and morrow' but for a full eight days, from which we can confidently deduce that the annual fair was by then a flourishing concern.

If the 'holy relics' had turned up in any other village in Huntingdonshire — perhaps one not belonging to Ramsey Abbey — would they have been greeted with equal enthusiasm and the place of their discovery promoted with such zeal? It seems likely that at best they would have been enshrined at Ramsey and their provenance forgotten. This is what happened to the Kentish princes. Their place of discovery is unknown except from Ramsey sources where they are said to have been brought from Wakering in Essex. This did not belong to Ramsey but it was part of the estates of ealdorman Ailwyn, the founder. So the attribution in the *Ramsey Chronicle* was probably intended as a subtle compliment to Ailwyn. There was, however, no practical advantage to Ramsey in Wakering and no suggestion, it would seem, of a shrine there.

Slepe was a different matter. It was the timely discovery of the bones at a Ramsey property with exciting commercial possibilities — on the great river Ouse and on land routes too — which gave the abbots ideas for its promotion. These ideas were only fully realised in the stability of the Norman period.

3   THE SHRINES

As we have already seen, St Ivo's discovery in 1001 or 1002 seems to have been greeted with spontaneous enthusiasm by the people of the local area. On his journey, 'translation', from Slepe to Ramsey he was borne by two abbots, Eadnoth and Germanus, 'like twin oxen of Christ'. The two were indeed used to working together as they had been 'outside prior' and 'inside prior' in the days of Oswald. As a former prior Germanus had been a candidate for the abbacy of Ramsey after Oswald's death but Eadnoth was preferred and Germanus became abbot of Cholsey. Other monks carried the other skeletons which had been found.

As they went a more innocuous miracle, of the kind shared with other saints, took place:

> Many of the faithful also claim that during the entire journey of this joyful translation a snow-white dove flew over blessed Ivo's remains, a miracle so widely observed that all would affirm the dove had come from heaven to favour the saint. A

crowd from Ramsey met with the rest of the people, dressed in white and crowned with purple ornaments, carrying before it banners bearing Christ's cross and Christian gilding, and splendid books of the saints, and lights on candelabra, and incense burning in censers, and whatever proof of devotion it could. The whole island echoed with songs and cymbals and the sound of bells; the woods and rivers were brilliant. In this way, with the angels rejoicing on high with the human choir, the precious pearls were taken to their promised temple.

On his arrival at Ramsey Ivo proceeded to give instructions for the building of a shrine there:

Ivo himself appeared by night to a certain pious brother and asked the father of the monastery that they would build him such a place as would be accessible to anyone who wanted to pray. Thus the holy body was brought back, and wrapped in precious cloth, and reburied on the way up to the sanctuary: it may still be seen there today, and be touched by eyes and lips.

The place of Ivo's discovery was not forgotten — it scarcely would be if the idea that Ramsey was alive to commercial possibilities is correct. And in this case it was the abbey rather than the saint himself who decided to build a shrine:

. . . abbot Eadnoth at the wish of all the brothers built a church in honour and memory of the blessed Ivo in that very same place of his burial and discovery. It was furnished in this way: the sepulchre with its restoring flow was half below the wall and half sticking out outside, so that whether the doors were open or closed there would be water of grace for people who hurried there. For the Lord is wonderful in His saints and He brought out a river from the rock; the tomb itself gushed with a healing spring, and the flow of this stream gladdens the city of God in His faithful people. St Ivo is very clearly, of course, in the tomb because as the waters of life once flowed as rivers from the innermost stomach of his devotion, so did the spring bubble up into eternal life, as he by his teaching and help had poured forth his fatherly strength to all men.

The next step was to secure the recognition of the shrines from the ecclesiastical authorities. Canonization only became a very formal process, involving the pope, in the later twelfth century. Before then saints could be made by popular acclaim. The procedure was for a bishop to make enquiries into any new cult, and Ramsey here had two advantages. The first was that they claimed to have found an old saint rather than to be creating a new one, which may have by-passed several awkward questions. The second was that any bishop would do—not necessarily the bishop of the diocese—and they could use a friend of theirs as Goscelin naively tells:

> Bishop Siward dedicated the famous church to blessed Ivo and his companions very festively at the invitation of abbot Eadnoth. Siward was the man whose worth as a soldier of Christ had been proved with brother Wilfred of Ramsey Abbey through deep perils of the sea and heathen nations. Together they were unconquerable by many persecutions and insults; they sought out a tribe and gained it for the Saviour, and at last, when their swordsman failed them, they returned to England.

This passage in Goscelin is actually a rather important 'missing link' in Scandinavian history. Sigurd, as the Norwegians called him, was an Englishman from the Danelaw who accompanied King Olav Tryggvason to Norway in 995 as leader of a team of missionaries. When Olav was killed in a grèat sea-battle in 1000 AD, Sigurd disappeared from the record for about eight years, resurfacing in Sweden where he was to assist another King Olav in the conversion of that country. He became Saint Sigfrid in 1158.

Another distinguished guest came from Eynesbury:

> The famous Ethelfleda was present at these gracious religious processions with a gathering of nobles. She was revered for her sermons, for her fasts and for other pious acts, and she had even founded with honour the monastery at Eynesbury and splendidly endowed it.

In fact this Ethelfleda is difficult to identify. She was probably Aethelflaed, the wife of Eynesbury's lay protector ealdorman Aethelwine who assisted bishop Aethelwold in refounding the monastery in the tenth century.

This ceremonial consecration, accompanied as it was by the earliest healing miracles, gave St Ivo of Slepe the Church's seal of approval and Ramsey now had two shrines for the price of one saint.

The new church at Slepe was maintained by a priory cell of Ramsey Abbey, where a few monks undertook a tour of duty (*conversio*) as the *Miracles* show. This cell was certainly established by 1017.

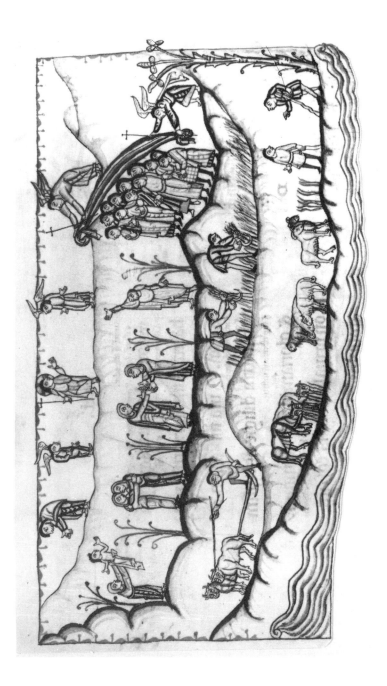

As has been argued, there is little evidence that Slepe underwent great changes in the early eleventh century. It was evidently a prosperous estate at the time of *Domesday Book* since its assessment was as high as any in the county. The village was assessed at twenty hides taxable with land for twenty-four ploughs and in addition demesne land for three ploughs. There were thirty-nine villagers and twelve smallholders along with sixty acres of meadow and an area of wood-pasture. Three of the abbot's men were named who held four hides of land for three and a half ploughs, and under them were five villagers and six smallholders with three ploughs. Two churches and priests were entered. There was no mention of market or fair but as such mentions were exceptional anywhere in the country this cannot be accepted as proof that there was neither. A comparison with the assessment for the borough of Huntingdon slows that Slepe was still no more than a largish village.

This would fit in with the idea that Slepe's major promotion was largely the work of abbot Herbert (1087-1091) who encouraged Goscelin to rewrite St Ivo's *Life*.

Herbert Losinga is an enigmatic figure. He was born in Normandy and became a monk and later prior at Fécamp. William Rufus brought him to England and he was elected abbot of Ramsey in 1087. He was there only three or four years, since in or before 1091 he was appointed bishop of Thetford, a position which 'his economy had enabled him to purchase'. There was a scandal about this case of simony, aggravated by his purchasing the see of Winchester for his father Robert. The interesting thing from our point of view is how he acquired the money. He himself, in all his letters and sermons, says nothing about his period at Ramsey. William of Malmesbury, writing in the first part of the twelfth century, says he managed the secular affairs of the monastery with consummate skill.

Certainly his career after leaving Ramsey reveals that he was an energetic and able administrator. In 1094, after making his peace with the pope and then the king, he moved his see from Thetford to Norwich, William says for ambitious motives — he describes Norwich as a centre of commerce and population. (The previous year Herbert had tried unsuccessfully to get diocesan rights in Bury St Edmunds, a move which shows he appreciated the value of a shrine as a source of income.) Once there Herbert organised the cathedral priory, which soon became famous for its numbers of monks, and he took in hand its endowment. He extracted valuable grants of land from Henry I, and also an extension of the fair at Norwich and fairs at Lynne and Hoxne. He died in 1119.

The conclusion is inescapable. Herbert Losinga had applied his administrative talents at Ramsey as he did later at Norwich. He promoted Slepe as a pilgrimage centre by encouraging the cult of St Ivo.

Part of this process was Goscelin's new *Life*: the versions we have begin explicitly with the dedication, 'Brother Goscelin to Master Herbert'. It is significant that no copies of the earlier life by abbot Withman have survived: it was evidently not a popular work, prized and copied by contemporaries. Goscelin's account, on the other hand, exists in half a dozen manuscripts today.

Another stage in the campaign at this time was the bringing of saintly reinforcements back to the Slepe shrine. It is described by the writer of part two of the *Miracles* which begins with the words:

> How in the reign of Henry the holy relics of bishop St Ivo's companions, after a three-day fast, were conveyed on 9th August back to the church where they had been discovered, by the brothers of Ramsey, and how many then were cured in that place

and continues

> At the estate, which is under the authority of Ramsey church, called Slepe, where once the bodies of holy Ivo and his companions were found after a glorious revelation of blessed Ivo himself and were transferred by the brothers to Ramsey with due honour, numerous cures of various illnesses were performed by divine intervention. Some inhabitants also of the same village claimed that they had clearly seen on many nights a ray of shimmering light reaching from that place all the way to Ramsey, sometimes rising up into the sky. The village itself was moreover not far from Ramsey, but about seven miles away.
>
> Therefore the brothers of Ramsey agreed, with the encouragement and advice of certain noblemen, that the relics (which had been stored together fittingly in a silver casket) of three of St Ivo's blessed companions who had once stuck inseparably close to his side, should be taken back to the church at Slepe which had been built in their honour. For then both the church there would be held more distinguished and more famous because of reverence for the saints, and it would be visited more frequently and faithfully by people from all over the place for the sake of the intervention of the patron saints there: also, the brothers added, it seemed right that the master would embellish by his presence the greater place he

had been transferred to; the disciples would adorn the lesser little place of their discovery. Indeed, lest they should appear to be going against God's arrangements in rash presumption, and detracting from the excellence or honour of the saints, they ordered that the saints' wishes concerning this thing should be sought with vigils and prayers and a three-day fast.

While this was being done a girl who was half-paralysed on the left-hand side of her body heard in dreams that she would be cured at the monument of blessed Ivo and his companions. When she had come there and had bent down for a time in prayer she obtained the outcome of her dream in full view of the brothers. They felt happier and more trusting after this sign, and when they had completed the fast-days and prayers, on August 9th, they transferred the holy casket crammed full of heavenly manna with praises and hymns and suitable reverence to the church at Slepe. Some brothers were appointed there by whose watchful skill the heavenly treasure would be guarded and divine service would be devoutly performed by day and night.

The influx of pilgrims to the new shrines encouraged the expansion of Slepe as a market centre and it is unlikely to be coincidental that the first permanent bridge was built in the next twenty years (by 1107) and Henry I granted the charter for the annual fair, which was already flourishing, in 1110. All the pointers indicate the 1090s as the beginning of Slepe's expansion and abbot Herbert as the man behind the promotion.

4   THE EARLY MIRACLES
VISIONS

It is convenient to talk about the *Life and Miracles of St Ivo* as if this were a single book, but it will be apparent by now that it is a compilation of different dates.

The first identifiable collection of stories is that of Goscelin. He was Flemish by birth and became a monk of St Bertin, a foundation which had a reputation for scholarship. He came to England in about 1058 to join bishop Herman of Ramsbury and Sherborne and he moved about as part of his household until Herman's death in 1078. During this time Goscelin undertook his first commissioned hagiographies.

Herman's successor, Osmund, was a protégé of King William and Goscelin evidently found him unsympathetic for he went on his travels in the 1080s. He came then to eastern England, visiting the larger religious houses and undertaking the writing, or more usually the re-writing, of their saints' lives. He stayed at Peterborough and Ely as well as Ramsey. In the 1090s he settled at St Augustine's in Canterbury and rewrote the lives of several Canterbury saints. He was still writing in 1099 and there is evidence that he was still alive in 1107 but the exact date of his death is not known.

Hagiography has been an undervalued literary form but Goscelin has generally been considered one of its more respectable exponents. Twenty-five works survive which are certainly his, and others more doubtfully ascribed to him. He was very learned, an excellent scholar and a skilful writer. Furthermore he seems to have approached his work in an honest and straightforward way, believing in the value of saints in a general way and prepared to turn his talents to specific tasks at others' requests. It would be wrong to dismiss him as a paid propagandist: his sincerity is quite clear.

Best of all, from our point of view, is that he treated his raw material with sympathy and respect — as can be seen in cases where the original *Lives* survive for comparison with his reworkings. At a time when other hagiographers were working to formulas, believing a person's sanctity could best be demonstrated by showing that his life and miracles closely resembled those of earlier saints, Goscelin was prepared to incorporate original and circumstantial detail into his writings. As a result of his integrity the miracles of St Ivo give us a unique insight into life in eleventh century Huntingdonshire.

There were various reasons for recording the miracles of a saint: the book was not just written for its sensational value, though entertainment might indeed be one of its functions.

Firstly miracles were written down to demonstrate the sanctity of their performer. This attracted prestige and indirectly endowments to the shrine and encouraged people to come from far and near to claim the saint's intercession.

A second function of miracle stories was to make a moral point. They often dealt with rewards achieved through perseverance or the exercise of other Christian virtues.

A related purpose was to discourage wrongdoing by showing the punishments visited upon people who failed in their Christian duty. The bailiff who called St Ivo's bones 'those of some old cobbler' and was punished with (probably) rheumatic gout is a case in point.

Goscelin's own idea of his job may be read in his preface:

Brother Goscelin to Master Herbert.

These things about the life of blessed Ivo have been recorded, which are known to have been glorified by the reverend abbot Andrew. He went on a pilgrimage to the Lord's city Jerusalem and spent such a difficult life that none of the faithful may hesitate to believe him. Indeed it is claimed that in Greece Ivo's name and life are held to be greatly distinguished by many deeds and miracles, and by the sweet scent of Christ's favours his reputation is very well known far and wide. Truly since his discovery revelations and marvels (which this Andrew my predecessor wrote down) have been proved as much by eyewitness testimony as by the evidence of the faithful. They have till now been written on the hearts of nearly all the Ramsey brothers, and several of the public, more memorably than in a book, and the monks are able to recount more vividly for writing down some things which were overlooked.

Therefore by the favour of our most holy Father, and at the request of all this most beloved and honoured community, I have compressed these things somewhat more briefly: in so far as it is easier to find what is being sought in a small work than among many things; it is quicker to arrive at a destination by a short cut than by a long circuit; it is more prompt to serve from a prepared little table than from a barn, and it is more pleasing to drink from a little spring than from a river. And yet indeed we have not made poverty out of plenty, so that one would complain that spice is lacking in this our abridged version: for in that other overloaded work there was too much; but enough has been used, so neither the more greedy nor the more fastidious may be offended.

> We have written these things about our most sacred father
> Ivo, very reverend abbot, for your loving and lasting remem-
> brance. We have acknowledged Ivo as worthy of the honour
> of your salvation, as first occupying the first position at
> Ramsey: and just as you have honoured and cherished him, so
> in the end may he take you for himself in the joy of his light.

Unfortunately it was not part of Goscelin's scheme to distinguish
between miracles recorded by abbot Andrew, which would be from the
shrine's first twenty years, and later miracles which were told him by the
monks. We cannot even assume that Goscelin used a chronological
order: the manuscripts have different orders and only a few of the
miracles can be dated.

Broadly, the miracles can be classified. The first and simplest group is
visions. The dove which accompanied the relics to Ramsey is one of
these. Another may have been a sighting of the aurora borealis by some
not entirely sober people:

> One evening some people of Slepe and others from the
> adjoining countryside, when they were lingering agreeably
> over supper and drinks well into the night, suddenly saw a
> very bright light in the red sky; they went out to investigate
> such a great omen, and saw flashing pillars of golden light
> piercing the sky from the tomb of blessed Ivo and his
> companions and illuminating the outlines of things far and
> wide... Therefore while they were gaping there at the celestial
> light, some of the bolder ones rashly hurried to that place of
> the light, but as they arrived it disappeared like a lamp in
> darkness.

The same explanation may hold good for another reference:

> Often a huge extent of light was seen openly across the sky,
> that is from the church at Ramsey all the way to the memorial
> at Slepe, which here swelled up, there sank down. There were
> also faithful souls in abundance who testified that they had
> clearly seen our heavenly leader himself, with a numerous host
> dressed in white, and he had revisited one or other of his places
> by way of a starry road, itself sparkling brightly with glittering
> ornaments. Generally, none the less, it was seen in broad
> daylight, a great procession of clergy and people following, all
> dressed in white, around the chapel at Slepe, and many
> candlesticks, and censers, and crosses, and shining banners
> were carried, which all proclaimed the supreme merits of the
> very famous Ivo.

These two celestial visions probably occurred later rather than earlier in the eleventh century, since there was a period of intense solar activity then which also accounts for omens and portents of the First Crusade.

St Ivo also kept up the habit of appearing to innocent bystanders and elaborating on his mysterious past:

> A countryman of Bluntisham reported one of these apparitions to abbot Eadnoth. He said that Ivo had often considered him worthy to appear to and be seen by, and that long ago,

appearing with his customary grace, Ivo had said these things to him, "I am bishop Ivo. About five hundred years have now passed since I found rest in my memorial at Slepe." Then when they heard this the brothers were curious and they read over the chronicles where they found it was the year 580 of our Lord's incarnation, when the heavenly flower Gregory was in his prime as pope, he who sent Augustine, the morning star of the English, to those who were sitting in darkness. So about these times the blessed Ivo is supposed to have gone over to the Lord.

Thus it can be seen how a mixture of innocent credulity and, perhaps, some element of attention-seeking fuelled the cult of St Ivo with tales of visions.

5 MIRACLES OF RETRIBUTION

However not all the people whom Ivo visited were blameless. About a third of the miracles in Goscelin's collection are miracles of retribution: as in the case of the doubting bailiff, the saint was quick to punish sinners.

There was a Norwegian monk who was on duty at the shrine of St Ivo at Ramsey who 'lapsed into apathy about his salvation, and he neglected the honour and reverence which he owed to blessed Ivo, or which it was fitting to display. For quite often as he crossed in front of the holy body he did not bother to bend his knee nor even simply to bow slightly.' St Ivo appeared at night and reproached him, which the monk found dreadful enough, but Ivo did not let the matter rest and had him whipped by one of his equally visionary attendants. 'When he told this to the brothers, his laziness abandoned, they became more careful of their own salvation and more devout towards God and St Ivo. And so it happens that when one is reproached many may be improved.' The monk Oswy of Ramsey was reproved more gently for omitting to say the psalms.

Other monks were punished in miracles Goscelin says were 'not of time long past' but more recent. One of these is interesting because the story throws light on a folk-custom of the time: a seasonal visit to St Ivo's shrine which was probably a survival of a pagan fertility ceremony. The fact that an Ely monk is the villain reflects the ill-feeling between the abbeys of Ramsey and Ely which is evident in several incidents in the *Ramsey Chronicle*.

> A certain monk of the Ely community was in charge of an estate under the abbey's authority. He ordered the villagers to plough, to thresh or to get on with other jobs on the one day in the year when they had been accustomed to come to the memorial of blessed Ivo and his companions, that is Slepe church, with sacrifices and gifts. One of their elders replied to him, "Lord," he said, "on this day all our villagers, along with the rest in the countryside round about, are accustomed to seek with prayers and offerings the support of blessed Ivo and his companions with God for their own safety, for peace and the earth's fertility. Therefore they ask you to put off to another day the work you have ordered." The monk, like Pharoah refusing to release the sons of Israel from hard labours and to let them leave his land in order to sacrifice to their own God, replied angrily, "Who is this Ivo, and where is his home, that you are eager to honour with such gifts? Who

he might be I don't know, and I'm certainly not letting peasants take a holiday from their tasks and go off to him."

But St Ivo in his usual way did not let an insult to him and his faithful people go unpunished. For when by chance the man who denied him was passing through the village of Slepe, made famous by the discovery of the saints, and as the monk came in front of the church dedicated in honour of blessed Ivo himself and his companions, he was weighed down with heavy sleep and said to those travelling with him, "I am too sleepy: until I have rested I can't ride any further." And getting down from his horse, he went to sleep beside the road, on the ground in the open air while the rest kept watch. And he saw in his dreams a man standing there, noble in stature, distinguished by his grey hair, magnificent in looks, dressed in snowy white, holding a belt in his hand and saying to him, "Do you recognize me?" When the quaking monk replied that he did not know him, he said, "I am Ivo, whom lately you said you did not know, and you forbade those who wanted to come to me. I have come just now to tell you who I am and where I stay." And pointing out the church to him from a distance he said, "Look, my home and the place of my habitation." He also gave him the belt which he was holding in his hand, saying, "Wear this belt round you: and with this my token remember well from now on who I am." And he encircled him with the belt and left.

The monk soon woke up, breathing heavily and feeling as if he had been tied round with a very tight iron chain, and told everything which he had seen in his sleep to his companions. With their help and with great difficulty he was placed on a litter and taken all the way to the estate where he had planned to go previously. For he was racked inside by a griping of his vitals; outside indeed he was tormented by a poisonous swelling of decaying skin: the flesh which the saint's belt had covered was rotting away. And because he was afraid of ending his life tortured in this way, he called his friends and relations to him and confessed that he deserved to be punished with such an injury because he had sinned against St Ivo, and he asked what task he might diligently perform in order to be made well. So they advised him to appease the saint's anger with prayers and gifts and to spend money on alms for the poor; also, over and above all this, to make a great wax taper, and send it along to St Ivo's shrine for his health.

When this had been done he gradually recovered and got back to his former well-being, and after his health returned he went devoutly to deliver thanks at the house of St Ivo, whom he had formerly despised, and thenceforth he held him in not inconsiderable fear and love, for Ivo was already known for his unforgettable token.

It may be unnecessary to point out that the monk's affliction is a classic description of shingles.

Another monk was in the company of a foreign abbot and he, having no time for such superstitions, seems to have been struck down by 'gippy tummy':

A certain foreign abbot, when he was on a journey nearby the place of the saints' discovery, heard news of the miracles done by them in that place and turned aside to the church to pray for their patronage. Then he also tasted the water of blessed Ivo's spring which flowed in the very same place where once his holy body had lain, and which supplied a health-giving drink to people ill with a fever, and he went on with the journey he had undertaken.

One of his monks, holding it worthless and reckoning it a falsehood, said it was not fitting for a wise and devout man to support the silliness or superstition of country people who, deceived by heathen error, worshipped the waters and the bones of any old dead people; led astray by certain imagined supernatural deeds of devils, they honoured them as if they were relics of saints many times proved.

He had not yet finished his words when he was suddenly seized by so great a weakness that he was scarcely able at long last to reach the place he was making for, that is Ramsey. There with a very severe illness he paid the penalty for his blasphemy, and after many prayers had been poured out before the body of blessed Ivo, because he had perhaps done wrong through ignorance, at last he was restored to health.

Miracles of retribution against lay people are even more interesting for the light they throw on eleventh century life. A rather touching one tells of Ivo's protection of a poor slave boy:

A certain slave, who had done something wrong and was terrified of an excessive beating from his furious master, fled for sanctuary to St Ivo. His master pretended to make peace and forgave him for his wrong-doing, but not from his heart. For he nursed his anger inside him and not long afterwards he falsely accused the slave of a crime and satisfied his fury by cutting him with fearful lashes, and between lashes he reproached him saying, "Take that one for Ivo; or if you like just run off to him again."

When he had said this, at the very same hour, he was struck down by a serious illness and took to his bed. Then when his survival seemed hopeless he summoned the slave boy to him and asked for his forgiveness. And having dressed him and presented him with his own clothing the master made peace with him, and sent him to the blessed Ivo to beg for forgiveness. When the slave had prayed to Ivo for him, the master recovered from his illness straight away; and then he did not dare to inflict on the boy, who had now been given his freedom, any insult or annoyance, but from that time on he was keen to fear and honour the blessed Ivo, because he had personal experience of his strength and power.

An intriguing incident which, like this, is in the longer manuscript of Goscelin and probably from the second half of the eleventh century, suggests gangs of Britons were intimidating the district. Whether these were descendants of the fenland natives who bothered St Guthlac earlier, or whether the term 'Briton' was used in a generally pejorative way, like 'vandal' today, we cannot tell and other sources do not help, but anyway St Ivo dealt with them effectively:

Once, when a wild and ungovernable tribe of Britons were rushing everywhere and ravaging Huntingdonshire, the inhabitants of Slepe took their possessions into the church of St Ivo and entrusted them to the saint. When the wolfish greed of the raiders got to know of this they hurried there in ferocious spirits, broke down the church doors and carried off everything that had been put there for safekeeping. But then one of them, looking about, saw a pair of bells hanging from the beams in the church roof. And coveting them he climbed up to take them for himself. Just when he put out his hands to take them down, he suddenly slipped and fell to the ground. All his limbs being broken, he died. When the rest saw this they were seized by a great terror lest something similar happen to them, and realising the holiness of the place, and paying tribute to God and St Ivo, they brought back humbly all the things they had arrogantly taken away.

Finally Goscelin quotes a very recent case of a local boy who made fun of the shrine:

In Stanton, a village very close to Slepe, there was a young man by the name of Alwold, who is thought to be still living. He came once to this same town of Slepe with a devout crowd who were flocking to the miracle-working tomb of blessed Ivo. He was not seeking health but faithfully seeking faithlessly to mock. The stupid boy did not know that God is not mocked but rather the person who is pleased to mock.

He put a snow-white hen on the holy altar, not as an offering but to stir up peasant gossip, as if she would settle there to hatch eggs. The boy was standing on his left leg and he bent his right at the joint onto his thigh, and shouted this in joking insolence: "Hey you, St Ivo, do you see that I am brought here stunted by illness? Why don't you put me onto the road to recovery?" He talked thus because he wanted to put down his leg and foot in the usual position and raise a laugh from the people by saying, "Look! You see a miracle, how your saint has cured me?" But in complete accordance with God's justice his pretended illness was made very real; for as he had bent, so he stayed for ever curved back stiffly. Then he believed indeed from true experience, and from true necessity; he demanded with deep groans what he had previously pretended did no exist—that the saint's holy power should restore him, now he had thoroughly learnt his lesson, to his former strength.

Poor Alwold never did recover and Goscelin's verdict is cold comfort:

>...great mercy was granted to the boy, since he was not suddenly struck down by lightning for rashly provoking the Lord, or banished, or dragged down to hell, but was saved by reproof in this world for eternal forgiveness.

Interestingly, an Alwoldus de Stantune features in a list of benefactors in the time of abbot Bernard (1102-1107). He gave 'the meadow upon which the bridge is built and the land from the bridge to the end of the ford.' If this is the same man — which is quite possible as he was still alive in Goscelin's time — then he made very handsome amends, considering the saint's intransigence.

The savage way in which St Ivo jealously guarded his shrine and his reputation, and the way these punishing miracles are recorded perhaps suggest an underlying lack of confidence. The narrator 'protests too much'. While the effect in the middle ages may have been to quell doubts, or at least the open expression of those doubts, to us the exercise of force suggests the failure of gentler methods of persuasion. Goscelin betrays the weakness of the eleventh century cult even as he portrays Ivo's miracles of power.

6 MIRACLES OF HEALING

More of the miracles are in the New Testament tradition and take the form of sudden and surprising cures. The classic disease for such cure is surely leprosy, and the section of Goscelin's work which describes the miracles begins with two lepers. Goscelin, though, often does more than catalogue the event: he describes the people involved and gives them human interest. The first leper is a woman and the story of her cure illustrates many of the features of a 'standard' miracle:

> A leprous woman, ulcerous, itching and bristling like a hedgehog with thorny prickling pains, had wandered all over the world looking for the protection of the saints. Then she came to St Ivo's health-giving tomb. She washed herself in the spring which flowed there by divine providence, and by her Christian perseverance, because the Saviour approved her cure on account of her faith, not long afterwards she cast off her leprosy, put on clean skin and flesh, and, leaving with her health completely restored, she made known to everyone the great works of God through his saint.

Firstly, she had been to many saints' shrines in her quest for a cure. This information was included to enhance Ivo's reputation by showing the failure of other saints to effect a cure. At the same time it tells us something about the duration of the disease. But its chief aim is to illustrate Ivo's power. It does not seem to have occurred to Goscelin that every time he uses this convention he is showing how low St Ivo's shrine was on the list of shrines to visit in search of a cure! In one case, as we shall see, a blind woman went from shrine to shrine for eight years before she got round to asking for Ivo's aid.

In the second place, the miracle refers to the spring which flowed from St Ivo's shrine. This is a feature of almost all of the healing miracles. It is supposed to have welled miraculously from the site of the shrine, and in reality it was probably discovered at the time the foundations were being dug for the chapel. Geologically such a spring is not extraordinary: the layers of clay and gravel give rise to several, including one which has given its name to nearby Holywell and can still be seen there. Belief in the power of water had been very strong in pagan times (and still lingers, as witness spas, wishing wells and the fountains in Trafalgar Square). The rite of baptism Christianised this belief. Saintly cures often used the power: usually water had to be used in which the relics had been dipped.

But in St Ivo's case, once again, circumstances favoured the monks of Ramsey and a natural spring provided unlimited supplies of health-giving water.

> The news of such a rare thing attracted the county of Huntingdon and its numerous people, because there emerged not only a clear spring from the saint's sepulchre, but even one which cured sick people by a bath or a drink. Who was not glad, either healthy or feeble, to take home from there a little bottle full of such healthful liquid, the feeble for healing, the healthy for blessing?

A third 'standard feature' of this story of a leprous woman was the fact that she was cured as a reward for her faith and perseverance. The miracle stories were intended to instruct people in Christian behaviour.

Lastly, her cure was not instantaneous. In very many cases it can be inferred that the recovery from disease was really a happy coincidence. This is especially true of leprosy, a disease for which there is even today no medical cure. It has been shown that the term was used in biblical times and in the middle ages to cover a wide range of diseases, including psoriasis and eczema. If the woman was suffering from one of these, spontaneous recovery would be possible. This is not to say the shrine did not play a part in her cure: a century's research has brought to light the importance of psychology in illness and cure.

The second leper is presented as a contrast with the first: a young boy who refused to accept his disease. He washed himself in the spring some five hundred times and challenged the saint: 'I won't give up until I get your blessing!'

It may be churlish to point out that faced with an authentic case of leprosy St Ivo seems to have been powerless. In 1044 bishop Aelfward of London had to resign because of his leprosy; his abbey of Evesham turned him away but his 'home' abbey of Ramsey welcomed him. The *Ramsey Chronicle* describes his arrival there — Goscelin is silent. It is important to remember that even the longest catalogue of miracles only records successes, which may have been a small minority of the cures sought there.

Blind people also used the water to bathe their eyes and regained their sight. Three are reported at the time of the consecration of the church at Slepe. A later case is more interesting for the light it throws on society and on pilgrimage as a way of life:

One man sent away his wife, having divorced her against the command in the gospels because she had become blind, which he considered her fault. She went in the direction of each and every of the saints' dwellings in the hope of recovering her health, binding herself by a vow and a solemn oath not to return to her own husband ever again, nor ever to marry another man, if divine pity thought fit to give her back her sight.

And when she had been around very many saints' shrines praying to be made whole by their illumination, for about eight years, then she groaned that she could never be cured. And perhaps divine providence gave heed to this, so that blessed Ivo might grant with greater glory something other saints had denied. Ivo's great and godly affection took pity on her sorrows, and at last gave her back the clear sight she had longed for. Therefore she was ordered in a dream to go on to the village of Slepe, to light up the home of blessed Ivo there. When she had set out according to the divine instruction, she poured out prayers and soon acquired her former eyesight. And now the new light made her more happy than her previous daily blindness had made her sad. For indeed delayed wishes are more happily received when granted, and things got with difficulty are held more dear. Moreover with her eyesight restored she set out with enormous joy and no one leading her, who had previously walked with such great grief and with another's guidance. And just as she had vowed, as long as she lived she remained in widowhood dedicated to God.

A case of deafness gives more details of the physical cure. It follows directly on the story of the lax monk at Slepe who was punished with a whipping.

That same monk had with him a boy who had been deaf for a long time, whom he absolutely loved. For indeed he had brought him with him from his own country, that is Norway, and had adopted him as son. He grieved with the boy for his misfortune no less than if he suffered it himself, and he never stopped battering blessed Ivo's ears with a perpetual prayer for the boy's hearing. Therefore one day when they were kneeling among the weak in the hall of the monastery, and waiting for St Ivo's help, suddenly the boy fell to the ground. And when he had lain for some time as if sleeping, and pus had flowed from his ears, he recovered his hearing and got up safe and sound.

This story also shows quite incidentally how matter-of-factly England was part of a Scandinavian empire at the time.

Two really dramatic cures of cripples are reported. The first uses very descriptive language:

> A man from the neighbourhood was bent and twisted so that he walked on all-fours, as would be more appropriate for two very little foot-stools. When this man had prevailed upon blessed Ivo in the place of his discovery, he was raised up, made whole, and turned into a biped. The brothers who were resident there in the saint's service offered him daily alms for a few days afterwards.

The second is longer and interesting because it suggests some pressure was put on the boy's relations — who were evidently wealthy enough to undertake a prolonged pilgrimage — to dedicate him to the monastic life. His initial unwillingness led to a relapse:

> In the same way a young boy from Hampshire, who had been crippled in his hands and feet from his mother's womb, was carried by his relations to the shrine of the martyr-king in Shaftesbury where he was straightened out as far as the hands were concerned. At St Ivo's shrine, indeed, he was restored as to the other disability which remained, and walked on his own. When he stretched out his loosened sinews while the brothers sang psalms, St Ivo appeared to him as an unknown man of remarkable dignity, who was eager to draw him towards him and to straighten out the bend in his knees, while in the meantime the boy, who found it unbearable, protested at the severity of the pain. Then standing on his feet and walking upright, and already giving thanks because he could go back to his family as himself, he encouraged everyone into divine praises.
>
> But yet one night when he had arranged to depart as a hired man according to an accepted agreement, or at least to escape the favour of learning which was perhaps urged on him, look what happened to him after vespers! He was attacked by an unbearable weakness, and he began to fill the walls of the monastery with loud shouts. And when the brothers, who put it down to his sins, kept on prostrating themselves for him in the chapel, the boy got his health back there, all his torments flew away, and in the same place, where he was now to serve the saint, he was taken in as a scholar.

Frequently the complaints cured were more trivial, though probably no less painful, and their disappearance more understandable. Several are interesting because of the people they deal with. Two of the earliest

afflictions were suffered by abbot Eadnoth himself (993-1006). He was cured of gout after washing his foot in St Ivo's spring and on another occasion he used a different technique to speed his recovery from an influenza-type sickness:

> Likewise at another time when he had been summoned to King Ethelred a very bad sickness attacked his entire body, and having taken over all his limbs it almost stole his voice when, look, remembering some brooches found with St Ivo, which he kept with him, he dipped them into water that he himself had blessed! After his shoulders were sprinkled with it the troubling and upsetting pain fled and the sick man rested, and refreshed by sleep he got up well and, a happy man, he blessed the Lord in His saint.

Another Ramsey monk, called Wlvard, was cured of erysipelas by application of St Ivo's spring-water. This miracle is quite unusual in that more mundane treatment has been tried first and 'divine medicine' only resorted to 'when he could not be cured by man-made eye-lotion'. Another cure in the community was that of a clerk's septic hand. This was effected by a different approach: he wrapped his hand in the cloth which covered the sepulchre.

Goscelin uses the tale of a cure of a Peterborough monk as the occasion to illustrate his detailed knowledge of the abbey's history. It was in the time of abbot Elfsige (1006/7-1042) that a brother called Odo 'was weak to the point of death with a pricking illness'. Then someone remembered St Ivo and a boat was sent (by far the fastest mode of transport in those watery fens) to bring back water from the spring. The monk, at his very last breath, had a vision of a bishop, drank the water and recovered completely. The cure of a Coventry monk does not really suggest Ivo's fame had reached so far, as the young man concerned was evidently travelling nearby:

> A monk of the Coventry community, Patrick by name, was making a journey, and he excited the horse he was riding on by rushing to and fro with youthful frivolity until suddenly it fell with him in such a way that he lay as if lifeless with fractured shoulder-bones. And so he was carried off to the nearest village. When at last a long time had passed during which he lay without speaking, he had an inspiration and remembered the miracles he had heard of which had been performed long ago by divine influence through the blessed Ivo; he was strong enough to find the words and asked that water for a bath be

brought from Ivo's tomb and poured over his bruised body.
When this had been done, he got better at once and as if he had
had not a single injury on his body, and he instantly set out for
Ramsey to offer thanks for his health. He planned also to do
this every year on the anniversary day of his cure.

The probable explanation of the monk's sudden recovery is that his
original injury was a dislocation rather than a fracture.

It is rather nice that Goscelin himself was cured, not once but twice.
Note the heartfelt description of his sleepless night when he had
toothache!

The author of this text, no less, explains that he fled for help to
the protection of this most merciful father when he was
twisted with gout both in the feet and the hands, and he
promised for the sake of his health thirty masses and the same
number of psalms, and so, when the fetters and handcuffs of
his illness were released, the joy of good health took over.

Afterwards as well, he reveals, pierced by a sharp pain in his
teeth, he spent a sleepless night giving out troubled sighs,
psalms and prayers; his rest upset and pain breaking out again
and again. He meditated painfully, then, at the time of lauds
he took himself to the healer-saint Ivo, and having delivered a
speech there, he bathed his limbs in the saint's consecrated
water and dipped in his mouth and teeth three times, and
directly, among fellow-choristers of absolute trustworthiness,
the pain ceased, and rejoicing in good health he proclaimed the
saint's power.

We have seen St Ivo inflict disease and we have seen him cure it. It is
perhaps time to examine mediaeval attitudes to sickness. The difficulty is
to conceive, from the security of the Welfare State, the insecurity of
health and of life itself in the middle ages. Examination of excavated
Anglo-Saxon burial grounds has shown an average age of death of 24 in
Kent, 31 in Leicestershire and under 34 in Norfolk. Fifty percent of the
population died before the age of 30; ninety percent by 50. People could
expect to be orphaned, widowed, bereaved. Illnesses we dismiss as
childish ailments were often fatal. Moreover the same examinations of
excavated bones show that most people who survived to middle age
suffered from arthritis and other degenerative diseases.

Nobody understood the causes of disease, so divine punishment
seemed only too likely. The complete ignorance of germ theory allowed
the rather worrying scenes suggested in the *Miracles* where one lot of

diseased pilgrims splash about in the holy water that others are eagerly drinking. Be that as it may, some illnesses, including temporary blindness, were caused by deficiencies of diet which might be remedied in the course of the journey to the shrine; others were seasonal and the passing of time alleviated the symptoms. Such relief would be recognised as a 'cure'.

It has been noted that 'cures' did not have to be instantaneous, which would allow some of these spontaneous recoveries to be acclaimed as miracles. Nor did they have to be complete: partial cures were recorded at other shrines. The cures did not have to be permanent: if the patient left the shrine 'cured' a subsequent relapse would not invalidate the miracle. Some of these temporary improvements can be put down to the psychological effect of the shrine.

The sorts of illness that would be susceptible to 'miracle-cures' include those which a proportion of people would usually recover from, such as shingles. Another group would be chronic or recurring illnesses where temporary remissions are a feature, such as rheumatism, which may account for some 'cripples'. A third category is psychogenic, that is real ailments which originate in the mind: paralysis, blindness and mysterious pains can all be psychogenic. Any of these sorts of illness—the relatively trivial, the long-term but remissive, the psychogenic—could be 'cured' by faith. A look at the stories in this chapter will show how many of St Ivo's miracles can be explained in that way.

7 AND OTHER ODD MIRACLES

There are a few miracles described by Goscelin which were not strictly to do with punishment or with disease. They include some of the most interesting.

Two different cases describe people 'possessed by the devil' and are very revealing of mediaeval ideas on insanity and evil. The first is of an elderly Ramsey monk. See how careful Goscelin is of his reputation:

We know an elderly monk of Ramsey, honoured and loved by all, whose name we shall keep quiet out of respect. Along with God's examining and His corrective scourge the name is bequeathed to the time of Satan (ie Judgement Day).

The glory of the first martyr Stephen distinguishes the day following the Lord's birthday: this day the old monk fell ill and was put in a cell in the infirmary. About evening he began to rave, to gape horribly, to gnash his teeth, to attack the people there with bites. Everyone was upset and rushed in; the hostile patient's strength was enormous; twenty men could hardly overcome him, and one body was not big enough for so many hands, so many hands could not be effective on one rebel. At last however he was subdued and, with his hands bound to his knees like a ball, he was knocked out with a crowbar. The pitying brothers blessed a large wine jar with water and put him in. The enemy's rage grew, detesting holy water more than fire. They hung round the monk's neck all sorts of religious charms, and the madness of the enemy was thereby increased rather than tamed and the devilish anger threw more gapings and attacks. In fact the man could not be set free there to wait for the power of remedy entrusted to blessed Ivo.

At last, on the advice of the brothers, he was carried down into the church to the saints' shrine. And as they were making for the choir through the chapel of God's holy mother, the man they were carrying began to sing out this Christmas song: "Blessed is he who comes in the name of the Lord; Lord God shine upon us." One voice of a friend hurrying to him and suffering with him chimed in, "Oh most holy guardians of this sacred cloister, come quickly to the aid of your servant's difficulties, and allow him no longer to be ruled by the enemy." The well-wisher was checked by brotherly arms, just as if he were bound, in the presence of St Ivo's health-giving memorial. Then indeed after he had hastily spoken, he took up the linen which had been placed upon the saint, and the cloak was ritually displayed more splendidly. The sick man shouted with unclouded mind and renewed health, "I see you and I recognize you, most holy father Ivo, and now I pray to you with a sound mind that your holy intervention will bring me full health."

As he declared these things in a rational manner, and persisted with calm feelings, the brothers suddenly released him from his outer bonds with great promptness on all sides. The free man was praying devoutly, and doing everything sensibly, and he gave quite surely proof of his deliverance. Who in that place was then able to cease from God's praises, when such a sudden calm had been created from an enemy storm? The sound of praise resounded through the whole church, and so did the offering of thanks from people blessing the Lord in His saint Ivo, and praising highly in great jubilation with hymns and cymbals. And so in this way, for the sake of our most delightful father, joy was restored more happily from this disturbance of the Lord's birthday.

At the other end of the monastic scale is a runaway novice:

There was a youth whose parents' devotion had led them to entrust him to the abbot of Ramsey to be directed to share in the brothers' life. He detested the rather severe rule of monastic life and tried to run away overseas, namely to Flanders where the school was that he had come from some time before. While he was working on this he went for a walk one day in a garden near the church and suddenly an evil spirit took possession of him and excited him and he ran to and fro until in a frenzy he ran into a house which happened to be next to the garden. The family of the house of course wondered sadly at his sudden madness, and held him down there with great force to see if the spirit would leave him. Almost at midnight or thereabouts when he had already started to get better, he saw two hideous men come towards him, who said to him, "Because you want to run away from that place of yours, we have come here to carry you off with us to the cloisters of hell." When he heard this he was roused and he sprang up and, once the doors of the house were opened, he flew swiftly to the monastery, shouting often "Kyri-eleyson". The brothers were woken by these shouts, and they ordered him to be caught and taken to the infirmary and guarded till morning.

When morning came he was distressed again. So the brothers ordered the priest to be sent for, and an exorcism for the calming of madness to be recited over him. But the exorcism could not be of any use, because the power of God wanted to demonstrate how great were the merits of blessed Ivo. So the suffering youth saw a person standing near who

looked to him like blessed Ivo, and the figure painted on him
the sign of the cross and promised him health in the future.
When he shouted this out with frenzied mouth to the brothers
who were there they brought him all the way to the patron
Ivo's health-giving tomb, where prayers were uttered for him
and a potion given to him made up of a scraping from the
tomb mixed with water, and in a very little while he was at
peace, with his frenzy calmed. Then, with the demon put to
flight, he was returned at the same time to a whole mind in a
healthy body and got up. And having thus been punished he
promised he would never leave the holy place to which he had
been bound by his father's presentation, and he took religious
vows and joined the society of the brothers.

In both these cases Goscelin treats the victim with notable humanity —
although the same could not be said of the monks. The belief that
madness was caused by possession by devils, and that these could be
driven out by violence or by magic spells is very clearly demonstrated,
along with different uses of the saint's relics: for the boy a potion was
made from scrapings of the tomb at Ramsey; in the case of the elderly
monk, also at Ramsey, the cloth covering the shrine was used.

A little group of miracles describes an odd continental custom, which
was to load a criminal with chains and outlaw him. He would go from
shrine to shrine looking for forgiveness, which eventually would be
evinced by the saint causing his chains to drop off. The first such
criminal described is a young Venetian nobleman who had murdered his
sister:

A young man from Venice, of the rank of count on his father's and mother's sides, and from a very famous family, was inspired by the devil to kill his sister, who was pregnant. Oh, monstrous grief of his parents! They could not avenge their daughter on their son, and for one eye blinded tear out the one that was left — for one eye suffer the loss of two. The bishop bound the culprit with iron chains; he was tied up with iron from his shoulders to his kidneys; his stomach and his arms were girdled with iron; and thus, handed over to Satan for the destruction of his body and the salvation of his soul, he roved through hot and cold regions of the world in suffering and hardship.

After a long exile, after various dangers, after visiting countless shrines of the saints, at last he sailed to Britain for the favour of English saints. At St Dionisius Parisius just one chain fell off; the rest were kept for blessed Ivo to loosen. When at last he came to the monastery of our holy father Benedict he was weak to the point of death: we believe the holy doctor arranged this so that he might be cleansed from his crime through the furnace of illness and so might be given bodily health and absolution. (So the Lord relieved the punished paralytic from his former sins, and soon said to the cured man, "Take up your bed and walk.")

Therefore on the feast of St Maur, who is the shape and likeness of blessed father Benedict, in the evening, when this verse of the hymn of God's holy mother was being sung in canon, "And His mercy is on them that fear Him from generation to generation," the young man in chains who was praying at St Ivo's tomb was suddenly seized by an invisible force, raised up completely from the ground, and then quite quickly put down. His iron bonds burst, not that they had been done up with a key, they had been made continuous. The chains themselves, once cast off, were scarcely to be found. Praise to the Lord, with songs and the ringing of bells, and with all the windows lit up, praise re-echoed in a loud voice of rejoicing! The miracle is correctly ascribed to blessed Ivo, with St Benedict and all the saints supporting him.

This account is not enough to tell of the young man, rejoicing thus in his freedom and complete health: with what humility he dedicated himself to his holy liberator; what thanks he poured out to the abbot and brothers, very great because they had revived him when ill with such great kindness; and, when the abbot had given him clothing to suit his rank, how happy he returned to his own country.

This miracle is followed by others describing the release of five Germans in total, criminals of baser origins. It is interesting to note these miracles of release all affecting people from foreign lands. It might on the one hand be evidence for the popularity of Slepe. . .it might on the other show how long the chains took to rust!

There is one other miracle reported by Goscelin which repays detailed examination. It was one of the earliest judging by its position in the texts. The story is a very circumstantial account of the miraculous recovery of a girl who swallowed a pin. Although it is rather long it is worth reading in full for the description of a wealthy Anglo-Saxon household and for the understanding way in which Goscelin portrays the father's dilemma:

There was a rich and faithful man in this neighbourhood, Godric by name, who had friends and relations in for a festive gathering. The walls were bright with coloured tapestries, the ceilings and floors were green with garlands of leaves, the couches were adorned with hangings, the tables with banquets, and the house, full of people reclining at table, was a riot of purple and gold ornaments.

His daughter, a girl as yet unmarried, was among the banqueters, and she was caught like a fish on a hook when she tried to swallow down a morsel of bread dissolved in her mouth. For by a hideous mischance a pin had slipped from a

young servant's dress, and had been folded in and cooked
when the bread was made. It stuck in the young girl's throat so
that it did not move, and nothing was left untried in the way
of devilish trickery; only the Lord could save her. There was a
bitter and pitiable struggle which was of no use to remove the
embedded barb or to make it go down. The rose of her cheeks
fled, a white bloodless pallor took over, her dying eyes failed
her as her sight grew dim. The inextricable pinpoint blocked
the entrance of life; death stood in the wings. Troubled groans
and faint sighs were borne away, and great anguish wrenched
loud screams from her instead.

The poor father rushed in; the mother hurried in, screeching
that she was wretched to have been preserved to see this day.
Then the table was carried out in loathing, the festivities
turned into lamentation, the lute became silent, and all music
was turned into grief. The idea of a banquet fell into ruin. The
father was confused by a double sorrow: both for the mortal
suffering of his most beloved daughter, and for the spoilt
happiness of his guests. The mother wanted to enfold her dear
child in her arms, to lean against her breast, to stroke her face
and throat with a mother's hand, and by crushing her to
comfort her in her alarm. But the girl, racked by internal pain
as she was laid out for death on her bed, was afraid of it then
because of a discussion among the Christians of her departing
soul! Oh, nothing is more frail than human strength, nothing
more destructible than man! Something so very small is big
enough to be the difference between life and death! Thus
stinging insects and gnats had conquered the Egypt of the
Pharaohs, and likewise in Christian times had overthrown the

innumerable chariots and horses of the king of Persia. But why do we hinder your decisions with many complaints, holy patron?

So, amid all these dangers, one man, remembering about the very healing water of St Ivo, was sent out on a swift horse, and a small draught of the holy water was brought back as fast as possible. Oh, excellent Lord, to whom nothing is incurable, who takes people down to hell and brings them back, and makes deep sorrow into joy! Suddenly when the girl drank the divine liquid the iron was dissolved and was extracted from the bottom of her throat; it came up and she had it all bloody in her mouth and spat it out. Then when people saw her as if revived from the dead, they shed as many tears of joy as they had before of sorrow, and everyone praised the Lord in His saint with suitable wonder.

Not long afterwards the daughter returned to the feast, very healthy with a rosy face, and the rejoicing which had been interrupted returned to everyone with increased interest. With what joy they were able then to exclaim, "Oh St Ivo, very great priest of God, what may worthily be spread about as your advertisement, you who brought up iron against the downward flow and forced it to come out and dissolve? May your glory bless the Lord of glory for ever!"

Of course it would be satisfying to identify the Godric of the story. It was not an uncommon name; however really wealthy Godrics are few. There is one possibility who is recorded in *Domesday Book* as having held land in Denton and Hemingford. The most likely candidate, though, had land in Slepe itself at an earlier period. This Godric was Eadnoth's brother and we learn about him from his will dated about 1007 when he left a wood called Acleya (Oakley) in Slepe to his younger son Eadnoth and land in Norfolk to acquit the heriot of his brother Eadnoth, abbot of Ramsey. Godric died in 1013 and between 1043 and 1065 his son Eadnoth and his wife made a gift of Oakley to Ramsey on the occasion of their son Aethelric's admission as novice. If the identification is correct it reinforces the picture of Huntingdonshire society as being a very small world in the eleventh century.

I think it is not unfair to say that St Ivo's fame was limited to that small world, at least in the period Goscelin wrote about. Most of the miracles happened to members of the Ramsey community, or people from the immediate locality; there was one affecting a monk of Peterborough, not very far away and obeying the same rule; other people, like the Coventry monk or the foreign abbot, just happened to be passing. There are certainly people from further afield as well: but in each case their resort to Ivo followed years of fruitless wandering. Just over thirty miracles are recorded in a period of up to ninety years. It is an interesting catalogue, but not perhaps a very impressive one.

8 THE TWELFTH CENTURY

Goscelin's book describing the *Life, Translation* and *Miracles of St Ivo* was complete in itself and ended with a little prayer:

> May he who has copied out these things devoutly and who has rewritten them, holy Ivo, concerning you, satisfy the Lord and you.

However in two copies the story continues with the translation of St Ivo's companions back to the shrine at Slepe (see Chapter 3) and then describes eight further miracles in some detail as well as describing others in a single paragraph.

The first describes a young girl who was bewitched. She is treated much more gently than the elderly monk and the novice:

> Also at another time while a young girl was busy gathering nuts with her brother in a certain wood, she suddenly heard around her something like a great number of different sounding musical instruments making a loud noise. She was terrified and made mad by these imagined demons' voices, and she lost her own voice, her hearing and sight at the same time. When her brother, who had separated from her a very short time before, found her thus wretchedly altered, he groaned as he led her back home.
>
> Afterwards as she was being led at her parents' wish to the place of St Ivo's relics and those of his blessed companions, seeing the church at a distance those who were leading her said out of pity, "Look, there's the church we are taking you to for healing, by God's pity and the intercession of the saints! If only you could see it and hear us!" Her reply soon came, "I do see," she said, "and I hear and I know I am in my right mind, and I give thanks to God and His saints for the restoration of my former senses." Wondering at such a speedy recovery, and praising the Lord together with a huge rejoicing, they went on their way more quickly to the place as they had vowed. When they had paid up their vows as pledged to the saints and given thanks, they turned back full of joy to their homes.

The complete cure of a little woman so crippled that she is described as spherical, and 'more like a monster than a human being' is recorded, then comes the case of Pagan Peverel.

This splendidly named member of the aristocracy has an authentic life-history. He accompanied Duke Robert of Normandy on the First Crusade (1096-1100) and after his return was endowed with certain lands by King Henry I, including the barony of Brunne (Bourn in Cambridgeshire). This led him at some point to lay claim to the villages of Stowe and Gretton (Longstowe and Girton) and brought him into dispute with the abbey of Ramsey. The outcome was a series of misfortunes for himself and his household:

One of King Henry's nobles, Pagan in name and Pagan in deed, surnamed Peverel, was misled by blind ambition and tried by a sacrilegious seizure to take possession for himself of two estates belonging to St Benedict's abbey at Ramsey, claiming falsely that they should rightly be owned and ruled by him, as much by hereditary right as by royal grant. But the brothers on the other hand were maintaining the testimony of many truthful men, that the estates had belonged to the church at Ramsey without restriction for a good while through the reigns of very many kings and without ever any objection or attack, and it seemed unfair to all and petty to the learned that after so many centuries of peace they should have to be given up now on account of some new and unheard-of legal quibble. But a mind deformed by insatiable greed once intoxicated by a drug hardly ever or never stops thirsting for others. For indeed this Pagan did not cease to suggest with bullying entreaties to the royal power that it should support his wickedness. But in fact the royal will could not be turned aside to wickedness, especially to sacrilegious robbery or the diminishing of the Church's property, on account of fear of God and reverence for His saints; but rather the king ordered the cases of both sides to be aired in a fair trial. Meanwhile of course with devout prayers the brothers entrusted their case and affairs to divine protection and the support of saints Benedict and Ivo.

The appointed day arrived on which abbot Bernard with some of the brothers, and many wise men of both sides, nobles and very powerful men arrived together at the village of Slepe in the burial place of blessed Ivo. But also men were directed there who were experienced and eloquent in judiciary power, to decide and define the case and what it was all about from the King's side. What more? After many subterfuges of the opposition, after arguments, with also the brothers' brilliant defence, the confirmation of suitable witnesses, also the testimony of letters from previous kings, the truth was clearly seen by the judges, with the help of divine grace (the intercession of saints Benedict and Ivo), and they decreed that in fair judgment the estates in question were under the authority and power of Ramsey church. The opposition who

heard this departed in disorder. However the abbot went back
delighted with the brothers to the monastery. And so that the
injustice of the others might be more truly evident, there were
divine miracles as a sign.

For on that same day, before Pagan arrived at his lodging,
the horse on which he was riding had its feet slip from under it
and fell three times to the ground, not without injury to the
rider, and a hawk which he was holding from his hand and
made for the wood in swift flight, never to return. The
horse of the priest who was travelling with him slipped
and fell as well, and its neck being broken — although the priest
was unharmed — it breathed its last. There was also Pagan's
steward, called Robert, who came in for a more deserved
punishment, because more than the rest, as it were the most
faithful to his master, he had given his approval and assistance
to the man's wickedness. Then his right arm from his elbow
right up to his chest and shoulder swelled up in such
unbearable pain that it was made much larger than his own
hip, and he could take neither food nor sleep, nor keep his
mouth in any way from terrifying shrieks and wails. And
when he was afraid of the danger of death from such wretched

torture, he had himself taken, conveyed on a waggon, to the church of blessed Ivo at Slepe, where he had recently done wrong and on account of this incurred such a punishment.

When he had kept watch in the church there for some days and nights to demand forgiveness with pitiable groans and sighs, he was regarded with divine mercy, through St Ivo's intercession, and at last he began little by little to get better; he was gradually restored by food, eased by sleep, and his arm lost its swelling. And then when he was able to walk on his own, he went fittingly to seek out the monastery of our distinguished father Benedict at Ramsey, and the health-giving tomb of blessed Ivo in the same place, to give thanks for his health and to be reconciled with the brothers against whom he had sinned. When he had arrived there devoutly and had sought and obtained forgiveness of his guilt in person from abbot Bernard and from the brothers, they guided him all the way to blessed Ivo's tomb. When they had prayed there for him and with him, and given thanks, and he had dedicated himself as blessed Ivo's servant for ever, they sent him back to his own people with joy, healed as much in mind as in body.

An equally long passage describes an unusual case of possession by the devil; here is a rather shortened version:

> There was a woman, mistress of a household, and when she had come to make hay surrounded by a company of her attendants, she went on a little way to a place somewhat apart, and as sleep came on suddenly, such as she had not experienced before, she stretched out rather unhappily on the cold grass. And when she had fallen quite deeply asleep the father of lies, the master of deceit, the source of all evil, to whom it is of utmost importance to overturn religion, to attack innocence — in short the devil — shot a poisoned arrow into her...
>
> A fat snake slid up to her easily and stole through the open lips of her sleeping mouth into her stomach, and it did not stop until it surrounded her intestines with snakish coils. .... Then the woman with this great misfortune woke up and perceived instantly what had happened to her. So she filled the heavens with loud cries, showing her grief in face, in gesture and in voice. She ripped her clothes, tore her hair, furrowed her face with her nails, and tried to commit suicide with her hands. Now she fell to the ground; like one of the Bacchantes, she ran around the grassy meadows with what speed she could. When the mowers saw this they were dumbfounded and made their way towards her swiftly, carrying their scythes with them in their hands, as if they would avenge the mistress of the household who they asserted had been overcome by a lurking adulterer. Truly this belief deceived them. And when the woman had turned towards the running men she forestalled them, and with tears welling up she spoke these words, "Take pity on me, take pity at least, my friends, and give me your weapons to kill myself. For my soul is weary of this life, which is certainly more unhappy for me than any death." Her slaves, who were now standing near, said to her, "What is the matter, my lady? What is all this you have just said? Why such an unexpected rejection of your fresh youth? And why do you keep pulling out your hair, which is your woman's adornment? Who then has thrown into confusion your fair appearance?"
>
> When she had outlined to them the pitiable thing that had happened, she was taken back to her own house with much wailing. Her relations and friends rushed in. But they who had come to lessen her grief, as usually happens, heaped grief upon grief. Doctors were also there, anxious as much as anything for profit; after many efforts, after long attempts, they went away perplexed and inglorious. And so the woman, lacking any human comfort, with everyone despairing of her

recovery, was sure (remembering to her own good) that she could be cured with the aid of the saints. Without delay she was taken with prayer to the most glorious martyr Edmund, whose parishioner she was as rumour has it, but she was not listened to there because, without ill-will, her cure was being kept for another.

Blessed Ivo's reputation was very famous in those days on account of numerous miracles. As the invalid heard this she entrusted herself to Ivo's patronage from then on, and, though scarcely active, she hurried with her household to the church in Slepe dedicated in his honour. There after two or three days of fasting, vigils and prayer she drank with very great devotion water from the blessed confessor's little spring. And it was done. When the internal course flooding in gradually drenched it with holy water the snake moved more sharply than usual. As it had not found rest inside, it was vomited up alive, a dreadful sight of course, in front of the high altar itself, in the full view of the many people who were there at the time praying for the woman to the Lord and St Ivo. And so the woman after a little while had her health restored and she recovered, as if she had never suffered the dangers of that or any other illness.

It is most likely that the 'snake' was a parasitic worm and that the scene in the hayfield was projected back from the final cure. It is nonetheless interesting to read the description of the mistress of the household leading her labourers in their work, and notable that she came to Slepe from Bury St Edmunds. The writer adds some verification:

Dearest brothers, the knowledge of this very great miracle was not brought to us by the report of just anyone, but by the conversation of those who knew the woman and saw the snake vomited up just as we have recounted; of whom some were monks and others very trustworthy laymen. So the bells ring out, the church echoes with hymns of praise, and since then even greater crowds of people flock to the doors of holy bishop Ivo, through whom the Lord condescended to perform such unusual, such unheard-of great things. To Whom is honour and glory for ever and ever. Amen.

This dramatic cure is followed in the manuscripts by a charming story about a spastic boy whose father was a gardener and probably in the employ of the bishop of Lincoln who had, even then, a palace in Buckden.

A certain stranger was staying with his little family in the village called Buckden; he was from overseas, a gardener by trade, and very poorly off. What is more, he had a son whom he loved very dearly who was eager to copy his father's skill with growing things and worked hard, but was paralysed. Of course his paralysis was very disagreeable and it disfigured his face, so that he offered a wretched sight to others, with eyes askew, nose crooked, spreading lips and his mouth almost curving from ear to ear without a break. The father indeed was not a little anxious about treatment for his son, and he spent out what little he had or could get hold of on doctors, but all in vain. . .

So one Saturday he came unawares (yet straying to his advantage) to a certain village which the common people call Slepe. This mean village, about five miles away from Buckden, is yet greatly renowned almost everywhere on earth for the greatness of the blessed Ivo and the frequency of miracles. When he had arrived there, and realised the reputation of the saint, he soon hurried to church with his son. Then, just like the taxgatherer in the gospel, he turned his gaze to the ground, fixed his eyes on the earth, watered his cheeks copiously with tears, and made a burnt offering on the altar of his heart which was most pleasing to God.

When he had been quite a long time at prayer, and had called on God and St Ivo on behalf of his son, he stood up at last, and deservedly he found his son, whom he had brought there paralysed a little while before, completely well, no doubt through the favours of blessed Ivo. When the father looked at the boy he clapped his hands in delight and, capering about in the way the French do, in a loud voice he blessed God as wonderful in His saints. Then, his mood transformed by the expression of thanks to the great and blessed Ivo, he returned home the happiest of men, whose arrival had been of the saddest.

Notice again the uselessness of doctors, which the snake-woman had also experienced. It is no wonder people clung to their hopes of a miraculous cure. But the chief feature of this story, as of the rest in this group, is the vivid way it portrays the people.

A woman from Canterbury is the next, chiefly remarkable for the distance she travelled to the shrine—though in fact she had never heard of St Ivo! She was cured of a vaguely described 'fever' as was a knight of Huntingdonshire. This man was in complete despair and only agreed to his friend's advice through apathy, and came to Slepe:

There indeed they fulfilled their vows; he with the fever fell asleep during his prayers. Not for long. He was somewhat wider awake, he stretched out his arms, and clutched his hood (for he had put on a cloak) more firmly; he also uttered a dreadful sound. "Why," he said, "such great injustices? And why do you strive to take away something which is not yours?" Supposing he was mad, his fellow-knight replied with soothing words. The other said to him, "In no way, as you consider, in no way am I mad. I know that, thanks be to God, I have been released from that restlessness which oppressed me by the remedy of the high priest Ivo — praise him in the highest, worship him in the highest. But listen, and I will unfold in a few words why the excitement which you fear happened to me so dreadfully. When I had lain down prostrate on the ground to implore God and His servant St Ivo that a remedy for my weakness might be given, suddenly a sluggish sleep stole over me unawares. And it seemed to me in a dream that my fellow-knights were doing military service with no small hired band of soldiers. I was serving with them as well in the armour of a knight. My foot was clad in iron, my head was covered by a helmet; a three-piece hauberk covered the rest of my body: at my side a dagger was hanging, my left hand controlled a shield. Safe therefore with these things protecting me, I despised the enemy's repeated attacks on me. Finally there was coming to me, as if I was seeing it in a dream, an image of most holy Ivo, namely that one which you may see standing on the altar. With one rapid move it threw down my weapons, twisted the three-piece hauberk on my neck, attacked me with a whip as I tried in vain to resist. Nevertheless I was still very frightened of enemy trickery, not understanding what was happening to me, complaining about the injustice, and I let out the shout you heard. When indeed the image had taken the hauberk off the back of my head, without doubt at the same time, through the favours of blessed Ivo — it has to be said quite skilled in healing — it took away all my weakness."

Therefore the name of the Lord be blessed for ever, who granted so much and so great grace to blessed Ivo, that through his image consecrated to His name such an unexpected cure could be worked. Amen.

It is a good description of a knight's armour and weapons. The statue of St Ivo, glimpsed perhaps in delirium by the knight, is probably the one described in a list of ornaments in the *Ramsey Cartulary* in 1143 when they were alienated by abbot Walter, without the monks' consent, in time of war. It was a 'statue of St Ivo, with gold and silver'.

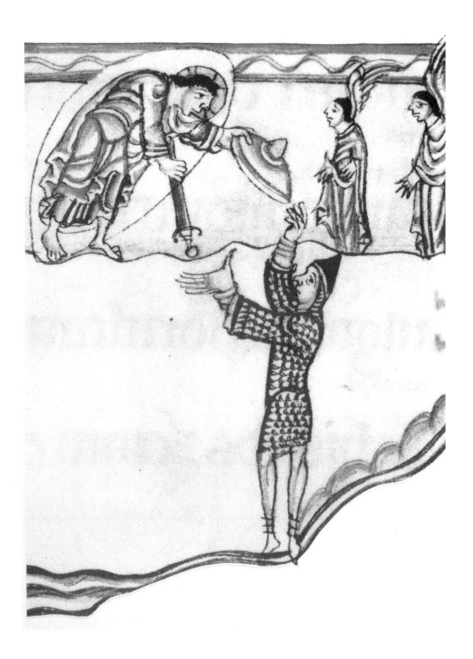

The last of these later miracles is incomplete and tells the tale of an undeserving monk, overseer of the priory of Slepe, who tried to talk St Ivo into curing him. We must assume that eventually he succeeded.

Although it is not impossible that Goscelin added these later miracles, as he is thought to have been still living in 1107 and the latest certain date is the Pagan Peverel lawsuit in that year, it is not likely. All the evidence is that he spent his last years at Canterbury, while these stories were certainly written at Ramsey. Moreover each story is self-contained: two of them end with a prayer and 'Amen'. The short sequence has the appearance of a series of records written up at the shrine and appended to Goscelin's collection. It was probably written before the date Ivo's statue was sold, 1143. The stories' being written within a very short time of the events described adds to their value and interest.

9   ST IVO'S REPUTATION SPREADS

So far it has been argued from the internal evidence of the various versions of the *Life* of St Ivo that his cult was mainly local. A search through the works of other mediaeval writers and sources does tend to confirm this view.

Florence of Worcester, who died in 1117, evidently had access to Goscelin's *Life*; the novelty of his account is that he worked out the dating and put Ivo's mission to Britain into the text at about 600 AD, rather in advance of St Augustine's arrival:

> St Ive the apostolical doctor, and a really inspired messenger from heaven and eminent bishop, departed to the Lord. His origin was in Persia, where he rose like a star in the east, but his course was divinely directed to the western regions in Britain.

He also commented tersely at AD 1001:

> The body of St Ive, the archbishop, was discovered.

The only independent witness to the vigour of the cult is William of Malmesbury. Around 1140 he wrote in his *Deeds of the English Bishops* about the two martyrs' relics enshrined at Ramsey, then he went on:

> Indeed, they are excelled in miracles, surpassed in signs by Ivo, bishop of Persia, who is buried there. One day he wearied of the pleasures which his very powerful see commanded and he secretly left everything to his people and set out with as few as three comrades on a very long pilgrimage. Therefore after a journey of many years, pretending he was a peasant with ragged clothing, he at last set sail for England. And he was very amused by the outlandishness of the unknown language, because everyone would laugh at him as if he were a fool, so he stayed in the muddy province where he spent the rest of his life. His companions died after him in turn as God foresaw. The provincials knew neither the place of his tomb nor the name of the saint.
>
> A long time went by, and the heavenly treasure lay in the darkness of oblivion. Then blessed Oswald left the earth, then Ailwyn made his end. Then, indeed, when it pleased Him, who measures out time and ordains all things in number and weight, St Ivo appeared in a dream to a man of innocent

simplicity, and he disclosed to him in turn his name and rank and the place of his tomb. Therefore, said Ivo, the man should go and explain his series of visions to the abbot of Ramsey and he should tell him to carry Ivo's body to Ramsey, leaving his companions where they were. His body was not to be placed in a special shrine, but in a place close to the altar, convenient for pilgrims. This vision was convincing enough to draw the abbot of Ramsey's belief. Just as he was slow to believe, so, once he gave his trust he was swift and prompt to acknowledge what had been ordered. So he went, and searched out the coffin, found it, opened it. And immediately after the saint's body was exposed, wrapped in linen, from those very folds of the sepulchre sprang a very plentiful fountain, bubbling swiftly. The spring remains to this day, sweet to drink and suitable for all illnesses.

It is not possible to estimate the number, much less to recount the stories, of the many people healed by that blessed one, so much so that no saint in England is more responsive to prayer than Ivo, or more capable of effecting a cure. I myself have seen that of which I speak. A certain monk was ill with dropsy. Now his swollen skin grew and grew, now his offensive breath drove away people standing near. It seemed he would drain all the rivers into him, emptying full wine jars. He was advised in dreams and went to St Ivo, and there, after he drank water for a third time he threw up a wave of the overflowing humour from his mouth. His stomach deflated, his legs grew thin again; and in short the whole man was rejuvenated in health, and at length he boasted that he could drink his fill of such liquid any time for the sake of such a healthy vomiting.

William's account seems to owe little to Goscelin. The saint's discovery has lost its opportunist aspect along with the ploughman and the bailiff's boots, and has become a more traditional missionary tale linked with a supernatural vision. The opening of the coffin (by the abbot) complies with the convention that saints' bodies were incorruptible. Ivo's companions stayed at Slepe rather than undergoing a double translation. William cannot have seen Goscelin's *Life* of Ivo but must have based his account on hearsay, perhaps specifically the words of the dropsical monk who had been cured at the shrine.

Henry of Huntingdon is interesting because he occasionally incorporated local detail, and nowhere more so than in his neglected 'ninth book' which was about miracles. He followed a conventional list of English saints—taken from Bede—with a survey of 'modern' saints and their shrines where books and information about them might be found. Thus he mentioned St Neot, then:

> Moreover on the same rushing river you may go and see the *Life* of Ivo, worthy of worship. For there the glorious body was revealed centuries after his death, in the time of the long-lived king Ethelred, who reigned thirty-seven years. This was not long ago from times we remember.

Although Henry, writing in about 1145, may have seen the *Life*, his words suggest he was writing down an oral tradition.

At about the same time—before 1154—part two of the *Liber Eliensis* was compiled, a book of records relating to the abbey of Ely. The discovery of Ivo's body is described in a passage concerning abbot Eadnoth (buried at Ely), but no details of the cult are given:

> a divine revelation was made to a certain smith concerning the body of blessed Ivo and about his companions also, resting with him at the village of Slepe. Appearing to him as a bishop, blessed Ivo said that both he and his companions had lain in that village since very ancient times and he ordered him to tell Eadnoth. The man woke up suddenly, he revealed his dream to the abbot and made him very joyful by showing him the

favour which had been bestowed on his time. Eadnoth did not suffer so great a glory of the saints to lie hidden in the mud any longer, but called together clergy and people and hurried to dig up the heavenly treasure with proper church ceremony. He himself carried blessed Ivo in his own hands all the way to Ramsey, others carrying the rest, and afterwards he built a church in Slepe in the saint's name.

This account of the discovery omits the more picturesque details in Goscelin but does not disagree in outline and may have been an abstract from the *Life*. It could equally be founded on oral tradition. It is interesting that these twelfth century accounts gloss over the finding of Ivo's bones before his revelation: perhaps Ramsey had by now decided that that order of events strained credulity too much.

The abbey's own version is in its *Chronicle*, which is more accurately an account of its benefactors and was compiled in about 1170. The story of St Ivo's discovery is told quite summarily: the discovery of the relics in a field on the Slepe estate near the Ouse by a ploughman; that no one knew whose the bones were until the saint appeared to a simple villager and said that his relics and those of three companions, yet to be found, should be taken to Ramsey; how abbot Eadnoth and abbot Germanus carried the saint on their shoulders to Ramsey 'where right up to the present day he works famous miracles'. The date of the translation is given as 24th April 1002, being ten years after Count Ailwyn's death, that discrepancy which was mentioned earlier.

There would be no need for the Ramsey chronicler to say more, firstly because he was presumably setting down information which was common knowledge and not anyway central to his purpose; secondly because Goscelin's account was available at Ramsey for anyone wanting the full story. Nevertheless it is disappointing that neither this book nor the fourteenth century *Cartulary* adds much to the evidence about the cult of St Ivo. (The *Cartulary*, or charter-book, has even more succinctly: 'And in the ninth year of Eadnoth's abbacy was the discovery of St Ivo and his companions at Slepe, and the translation of those same saints was in the same year.')

Just before the end of the twelfth century John of Brompton wrote of Ivo's discovery. His account describes Ivo (and his three companions) settling to live the life of a hermit on the isle of Ramsey, and later appearing to a simple man in a dream urging the abbot to disinter him. A fountain springs from the tomb and John finishes: 'it is so healthy that even today there is hardly a saint in all England more responsive to prayer than St Ivo, or more capable of effecting a cure.'

The similarity of wording puts it beyond doubt that John of Brompton was condensing William of Malmesbury. The only slightly surprising thing about this is that there was a copy of the *Life* at Jervaulx, where John is believed to have worked, and he might be expected to have seen it.

Another John, of Wallingford, has been credited with the authorship of a chronicle which, however, was written about 1220 by someone else. This chronicle contains a history of Britain from Brutus to Cnut and incorporates saints' lives chronologically. There is a very full account of Ivo's 'life' and discovery which in places echoes Goscelin closely. It has the date, 1001, the disciple Patricius and another hermit who was buried with him. However they were in their graves three hundred years, not four. The prophecies of the old man in Rome are quoted. The ploughman has become a farmer and he reports the find:

> When the matter had been reported, a monk named Ethelnoth ran up, to whom it was evident from the prophecy that relics of saints were in that village. Therefore he had the saints, duly washed, taken to the little village church, and he placed them with some honour next to the altar; and he left them there until he knew both the name and the merits of the person whose relics they were (he had decided to find out through the prayers of the brothers). God's mercy was not lacking for long on this score: for St Ivo appeared to a certain smith . . .

The vision of the smith is almost word for word the same as in Goscelin but the recipient of his tale has undergone a transformation:

> Next morning straight away he announced to Eadnoth the vision he had seen, but Eadnoth rejected the story as fantastic and added: "should we translate the miserable ashes of some cobbler and honour them as saints?" Thus the simple man withdrew in embarrassment, but nevertheless he was at once freed from the pain of the blow. Indeed the following night the saint appeared to Eadnoth in dress and aspect just as the smith had approached Eadnoth to tell him, and Ivo made this terrible beginning: "Get up!" he said, "Get up! . . ."

That John believed it was the abbot who was punished is borne out by his final sentences:

Then he woke up to feel himself attacked by gout, and he returned to the monastery and preached those things which he had refused to believe before, or believed unwillingly. Moreover after a short while he had the two companions of Ivo, about whom he had received orders via the smith, disinterred, and had them translated with honour to Ramsey at the same time as St Ivo.

It is a rather curious mistake, for Goscelin is unambiguous about bailiff and abbot and confusion is only likely when we know—as the *Ramsey Chronicle* tells us but Goscelin does not— that both men were called Eadnoth. Moreover the chronicler is generally well informed about Ramsey and has information about Eadnoth's co-prior Germanus which is found nowhere else. The error illustrates the vagaries of survival which affect our mediaeval sources. The author almost certainly copied or excerpted from a *Legenda Sanctorum* (Book of the Saints) which is now lost, and in the transmission errors have crept in.

The John of Wallingford who did not write the chronicle attributed to him was a friend and admirer of a much better known writer, Matthew Paris. He repeated the confusion of abbot Eadnoth with bailiff Eadnoth in his *Great Chronicle*:

> In the same year (1002) St Ivo was found not far from Ramsey Abbey, and because the abbot of Ramsey had not respectfully accepted his discovery he was severely punished.

(In his *History of the English* he had a longer version which, however, adds little information.) Writing of his own times he again referred to the shrine of St Ivo:

> In the same year also (1250) three Armenian brothers, who had fled when expelled by the Tartars from the lands of their birth, came to St Ives to pray there, for blessed Ivo had been oriental by birth. They had bearded faces and were venerable men in deeds and in sanctity. There also one of them, named George, who seemed to be their chief, was carried off by illness and he left the world in a very pious manner; and because he was believed to have been a bishop, as far as could be gathered from his companions who were foreigners, he was reverently buried next to the church, where he even began to work bright miracles.

What a splendid irony! How unfortunate that Ramsey no longer needed a saint: this George—whose two companions must have been rather bemused by events—sounds quite as convincing as St Ivo.

There is another kind of documentary survival which may be set alongside the literary evidence. This is the Kalendars of the English Benedictine monasteries. These recorded the festivals of the Christian year and reflected local customs and patronage. Twenty survive from before 1100 and St Ivo does not appear in one. The list includes Ely and Crowland, but not Ramsey itself, nor Thorney nor Peterborough.

Eighteen kalendars after 1100 have been found and two festivals relating to St Ivo are in some of these. His discovery on 24th April was celebrated at Ely, Crowland and St Albans; his translation to Ramsey, on 10th June, was noticed at Ely and (for some unknown reason) at Westminster. The survivals are too random to prove anything on their own, but they may be added to the weight of evidence. A related monastic source is the relic-list. Of those which survive (Ramsey's does not) only St Albans and Salisbury claimed to have relics of St Ivo. A twelfth century martyrology from Exeter has St Ivo—though he was scarcely a martyr!

The fact that St Ivo appears in surviving kalendars and relic-lists of St Albans is explained by the travels of another Huntingdonshire religious: a woman who started life as Theodora of Huntingdon but became Christina of Markyate. Markyate was a daughter foundation of St Albans and Christina was abbess there during the first half of the twelfth century. A copy of her psalter can be seen which has added in various 'obits' all to do with her family and friends. The kalendar in it has been altered to include some female saints and also St Felix and St Ivo, both connected with Ramsey. Once again, apparent evidence of an influential cult turns out to have origins very local to Slepe.

There is, of course, a degree of chance attached to the survival of any mediaeval writings. We have to assume, if we are to deduce anything at all, that the more frequently read and copied manuscripts were most likely to survive, so that what we have today is fairly representative of the sort of coverage St Ivo received in the middle ages. All the written evidence seems to support the conclusion that St Ivo's cult was never widespread.

Interest in St Ivo seems to have been at its height in the twelfth century and to have declined thereafter. His name might have been forgotten completely if it had not become inextricably linked with the annual fair at Slepe. In the charter of 1110 Henry I granted the Easter fair to 'St

Benedict of Ramsey and St Ivo of Slepe' and it seems to have been known straight away as 'St Ivo's fair'. In the charter settling the Pagan Peverel case the abbot's court was *'apud Sanctum Yvonem'*, or 'at St Ive's place'. Henry II's confirmation charter 1154/1160 is headed *'De feria de Sancto Yvone'* — 'concerning St Ive's fair' and in his reign also individuals begin to crop up with *de Sancto Yvone* (of St Ives) as distinguishing name or surname. Thus the emphasis shifted until Slepe was forgotten and the growing town was known only as St Ives. The chronicle attributed to John of Wallingford, written about 1220, is explicit: 'In 1001 AD St Ivo, archbishop and confessor, was found on an estate of Ramsey church which used to be called Slepe, but nowadays indeed it is known by the name of the saint.'

Thus the whole promotion campaign which gathered momentum towards the end of the eleventh century had achieved a rare degree of success: it not only made the village of Slepe a flourishing commercial centre, it also immortalized its 'front man', St Ivo, in a way which was probably quite unforeseen.

10   THE END OF THE STORY

The origins of fairs go back beyond recorded history, but many or most are believed to have developed from gatherings for pagan or Christian festivals, often associated with holy wells. The Slepe fair was granted for Easter week, which fits in with this idea, as does the record (in the story of the Ely monk) that villagers were accustomed to come from some distance to ask St Ivo to give peace and fertility to the land, a custom which may have developed from a well ceremony in pagan times. The annual fair probably predated the discovery of the relics, therefore, and provided a ready framework for their exploitation.

If Slepe had developed as an annual trading centre, this was because of notable natural advantages: it was readily accessible by water, including the river Ouse which was navigable by continental merchants; roads concentrated overland traffic at the ford and provided for exchange between the east coast and the midlands. Ramsey Abbey would have been very unworldly not to have realised that Slepe offered much better prospects for commerce than Ramsey itself, surrounded by fenland and accessible by road only from the south.

Making the village a shrine was undoubtedly a money-spinning idea, but one that was not fully realised in the eleventh century, perhaps because Eadnoth was so soon promoted to bishop and Andrew, who is the next known to have taken an interest in the saint, was distracted by the idea of a pilgrimage elsewhere. His legacy, a life of St Ivo, was apparently rather impenetrably written. It took the Norman, Herbert Losinga, to realise the potential of the connection between cult and fair, and thereafter they were interdependent.

The fair prospered exceedingly, reaching a peak in the thirteenth century when Henry III extended its duration to four weeks and Edward II allowed a full forty days, ending on the eve of Pentecost. Its prosperity brought Ramsey Abbey into conflict with other authorities. In 1252 there was a dispute with the king's bailiffs who claimed the king should receive the benefit of the extra three weeks' revenues. The abbot claimed he had charters of Edgar and Edward which had been confirmed by Thomas a Becket, but they did him no good and he was deprived of the fair 'to his church's enormous damage and loss' (Matthew Paris). He stated that the value of the fair to the abbey exceeded that of several manors. The grant was renewed in 1258 but a further long-running dispute developed with the burgesses of Huntingdon about tolls, and this lasted from 1260 to 1286. Nevertheless in 1268 merchants sailed to St Ives from Ypres, Poperinghe, Ghent, Brabant, Malines, Amiens and St Omer, Artois, and Douai, and there they traded with merchants especially from Lincoln, Beverley and Leicester who hired entire rows of booths or houses.

The decline of the fair seems to have begun at the very end of the thirteenth century when, it has been noted, the court records have many fewer names in them. It has been suggested that competition from Sturbridge fair, just outside Cambridge, may have been instrumental in this decline, but it is more likely that the two complemented and enhanced each other's trade, since Sturbridge was an autumn fair. Its dependence on overseas merchants certainly meant that the Hundred Years' War (1336-1431) was fatal to St Ives. Disruption to trade and the imposition of heavy taxation followed its outbreak. Then the Black Death swept Europe in 1348 and 1349, causing social upheaval and economic unrest. The fair never fully recovered, though it exists today in a very attenuated form.

The priory had developed — always as a dependent cell of Ramsey — alongside the fair, receiving grants of land, such as that of Alwold on which the bridge was built. The priory church of 1017 was burnt down in 1207 but was rebuilt and dedicated in 1237 or 1238. The monastic strength at St Ives' peak is not known, but by 1439 there was only a prior and two or three monks, and exactly a century later when the priory was dissolved only one monk, the prior, received a pension. The priory's worth in 1535 (*Valor Ecclesiasticus*) had been put at just over £9.

Like the fair, the legend of St Ivo lived on in debased form. It was one of the *Lives* collected and rewritten by John of Tynemouth in the fourteenth century. He apparently worked from the 'Goscelin plus' version of the story and offers an abridged form. Thus he has Ivo's exotic origins; his discovery; the dreams (the smith is called Ezi, the bailiff Elnoth); his translation; the date 600 AD; the shrines; the two lepers, the negligent monk, the Venetian and the Germans freed from their chains, the divorced wife, Alwold of Stanton, the Ely monk and the runaway novice. There follows a general testimonial to the efficacy of St Ivo's spring, then three rather silly miracles not found in earlier accounts. The first concerns a merchants' servant:

> A certain boy, eagerly filling for them a cooking pot given to him by some merchants his masters, put into it water drawn from the saint's tomb, and lit a big fire: yet when the meats were served to the reclining diners they were found to be raw and full of blood. This thing had to be explained, for the water in the pot was found to be absolutely cold: St Ivo's water stays always the same; it knows no deterioration, nor suffers any eclipse; and any time it is drunk rather greedily in great quantity, it never brings any illness to the drinker, nor blows up his belly.

This is followed by the unpleasant story of a woman who used to copulate with the devil in the guise of a hare. She confessed to the prior of St Ives and was given a phial of water from St Ivo's spring which preserved her from further sin.

Another woman may remind us of her predecessors who arrived at St Ives as a last resort. She got part of her cure from St Thomas of Canterbury so the story cannot be earlier than 1170:

> A certain woman, blind from birth, doing the rounds of the saints all over England, was returning from blessed Thomas the Martyr and was on her way to seek the help of St Ivo when she approached a small hill near his village. She sank down wearily and fell asleep for a little while. Two splendid men were there in bishops' robes (one coming along the road she had used; the other along the road she was going to use), and they were carrying in their hands two eyes shining brightly (as it seemed to her): one fitted the eye he held into her head; the other fitted the other. When the woman woke up she rejoiced to have gained her eyes and her sight: moreover no one doubted that this miracle should be attributed to the blessed martyr Thomas and St Ivo.

A brief reference to three men bloated by dropsy who were cured ends the account rather abruptly. All in all John of Tynemouth adds very little to our knowledge of the cult. If the four miracles cited above are the sum total for some two centuries then clearly the cult was past its heyday. Perhaps this may reflect a more widespread decline: the age of the minor saint was over and pilgrimages had become big business — package tours to the major centres such as Walsingham and Canterbury (as in Chaucer). Other centres came and went in the fourteenth century as Jusserand points out in his *English Wayfaring Life*:

fashion ruled as mistress; some relics or tombs of hermits or of saints enjoyed for a period universal favour; then all of a sudden, through some great miracle, another saint rose to pre-eminence, and his rivals, by degrees, dwindled into obscurity.

But St Ivo's decline was also linked with the decline of his fair.

St Ivo's cult seems never really to have caught on outside the very local area. There is indeed an odd case of witchcraft which reached the courts in London in 1528 when one Margaret Hunt admitted to using charms for healing. When the sick people went to bed at night they were 'to sey one pater, one ave and one crede in the worshypp of Seynt Ive, to save them from al envy . . .' This spell had been learnt in Wales from a woman called mother Emet. The 'Ive' concerned could have been a Celtic saint, though the context of healing suggests it is ours.

The Celtic 'St Ive's confuse matters in Cornwall where there are two settlements. The larger one in West Cornwall is really named for a Celtic saint, St Ia or Hya, an Irish virgin. It was called St Ie's until the sixteenth century when 'St Yves' is found. It is suggested that Breton influence is responsible for the 'v' since sailors may have confused the patron with the more famous Breton saint, Yves Hélori of Tréguier (1253-1303).

The second village is St Ive near Liskeard in East Cornwall. The settlement was probably originally named for a Celtic saint, perhaps the Welsh John (Ivon). The parish was held by the Knights Templars and it could have been they who, arriving from regions where St Ivo of Slepe had achieved some reputation, assumed that the dedication referred to him. They may also have been misled by an analogy with St Neot (near St Ive in Cornwall) and St Neots (near St Ives in Huntingdonshire), since the coincidence is so striking. By 1291 the church was referred to as *Ecclesia Sancti Ivonis* in a papal document.

One other dedication to St Ivo is found at the other end of England, at Leadgate in County Durham. This is strange because the parish was only formed in 1863 and the church consecrated in 1867. However the dedication is based on a local tradition. A small village called Iveston is within the parish and it has a large boulder on its boundary which is known as St Ive's stone because St Ive is supposed to have preached on it and has, indeed, left his footprints upon it. It was the custom in the early nineteenth century for villagers to meet there at the end of harvest and for one of them to mount the stone and hold forth. Whether the legend originated in anything more than a coincidence of names is impossible to say. It has been suggested that as the village lies midway between the two

Roman camps of Ebchester and Lanchester, which drew soldiers from the East, Ivo may have preached there to the colonists' descendants. Rather far-fetched, but no more so than the rest of St Ivo's story!

Finally, St Ivo found his place in *1066 and All That* where there is 'a Wave of Saints. Among these were St Ive, St Pancra, the great St Bernard (originator of the clerical collar), St Bee, St Ebb, St Neot (who invented whisky), St Kit and St Kin, and the Venomous Bead (author of *The Rosary*)'.

As this is 'the only Memorable History of England' how right that St Ivo should figure in it.

APPENDIX ONE
Manuscripts and editions

The original account of the *Life and Miracles of St Ivo*, by abbot Andrew, has not survived. The inference is that there was just one copy at Ramsey and this was lost or destroyed after its use by Goscelin. It is difficult to know how much of the original was incorporated into Goscelin's account, and how much of his information is oral tradition, which he asserts he has used.

We do not have Goscelin's autograph *Life* but two copies are extant. One of these is in the British Library: *MS Cotton Tiberius D.iii, ff241v-248r* (D). It is a twelfth century copy in a handwriting that would be easily legible had not the volume been involved in the disastrous Cotton fire of 1731 after which, as the catalogue says, it was 'burnt to a crust and preserved in a case'. Parchment is, however, much tougher than paper and expert remounting has allowed close examination of the manuscript. This shows that the copy is very closely related to one in Dublin (T): so much so that both refer to the village as 'Splepe' on its first appearance! The main difference is not in content but in organisation, and that is only slight. D has the chapter headings listed at the beginning and thereafter uses numbers only to signal the start of new chapters in the text; T has the chapter headings incorporated into the text. D is evidently older but its history before Cotton acquired it is not known. It contains a miscellany of saints' lives, of which Ivo's is the last.

The Dublin manuscript (T) is *Trinity College 171* and it was previously owned by, probably written at, Jervaulx Abbey in Yorkshire. Again the saint's life is one of many, though the mixture is different. T is in a good thirteenth century hand and occupies pages 230 to 250 of the book. Both of these manuscripts begin with Goscelin's prologue and go on to describe Ivo's origins, his discovery, the dreams, the date, his translation to Ramsey, the prophecies and the building of the shrines. There are fewer miracles and in a different order from later versions: the leprous woman; the leprous boy; the church dedication; the blind woman; Eadnoth (2); Godric's daughter; lights in the sky; the Bluntisham man; Oswy of Ramsey; more visions; prisoners freed (3); the boy from Hampshire; the author's gout and toothache; the Peterborough monk; the Fenstanton youth; the elderly Ramsey monk; closing words.

The version preserved in these two manuscripts begins with Goscelin's elaborate prologue and has nothing in it which disagrees with a date of circa 1090, and therefore I have treated it as being the *Life of St Ivo* as written by Goscelin at that date.

Two manuscripts are extant which contain the same text as Goscelin but with lengthy additions. The more important is in Oxford, *MS Bodley 285* (B). This dates from the first half of the thirteenth century and was almost certainly written in and for Ramsey Abbey. It has *Lives* of Sts Ivo, Ethelred and Ethelbert, Oswald and Dunstan, which supports the theory of Ramsey provenance. A second copy of 'Goscelin plus' is in Douai, *MS 852* (C). This is also a thirteenth century manuscript and was originally owned by Crowland Abbey. It was either copied from B or they were both copied from the same original. Two variations prove that it is not an earlier version: B has the same wording for the Peterborough monk as the two Goscelin manuscripts while C has greatly abridged the tale, cutting out all the information on Peterborough's history. The copyist may have intended to spare his readers much tedium or the omission may have resulted from rivalry between the abbeys of Crowland and Peterborough. The second omission is the story of the author himself being cured of gout and toothache. In this case a guess is that the writer had scruples about claiming a cure 'himself' which had happened to someone else.

These two miracles are also included out of sequence in B. The manuscript has St Ivo's origins first, *'In civitate Frianeos...'*, then follows the same order as Goscelin up to and including Eadnoth's afflictions. The Peterborough monk follows, then Godric's daughter, then the author's cures. Two new stories follow: erysipelas and the Coventry monk, then three from Goscelin (lights, Bluntisham man and Oswy of Ramsey), then three more new ones: the quadruped, the negligent monk and the deaf Norwegian boy. The sequence, visions — prisoners freed — boy from Hampshire, is as in Goscelin; septic hand and divorced wife are interpolated; the Fenstanton youth comes next; the monk of Ely, the foreign abbot, the slave boy and marauding Britons are inserted; the elderly Ramsey monk is as in Goscelin; the runaway novice is inserted, then the closing words are written exactly as they are in Goscelin.

None of these miracles is necessarily later than the date Goscelin wrote and one or two of them have the character of being earlier rather than later eleventh century: the marauding Britons and the Norwegians sound pre-Conquest. This part of B may be a rearrangement of Goscelin,

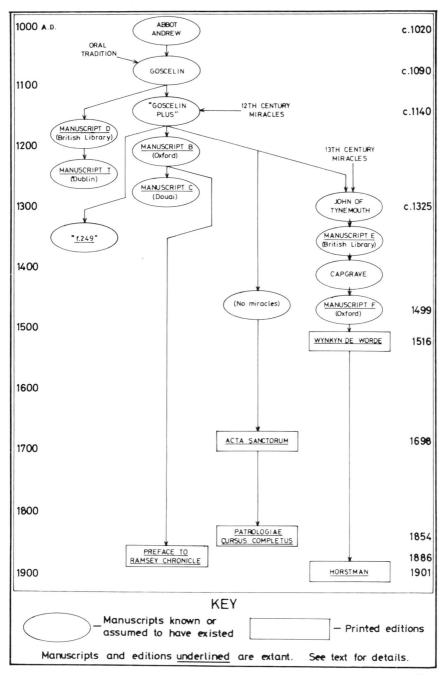

1000 A.D.	ABBOT ANDREW	c.1020
	ORAL TRADITION → GOSCELIN	c.1090
1100		
	"GOSCELIN PLUS" ← 12TH CENTURY MIRACLES	c.1140
	MANUSCRIPT D (British Library)	
1200	MANUSCRIPT B (Oxford)	
	MANUSCRIPT T (Dublin)	13TH CENTURY MIRACLES
	MANUSCRIPT C (Douai)	
1300	JOHN OF TYNEMOUTH	c.1325
	"f.249" MANUSCRIPT E (British Library)	
1400	CAPGRAVE	
	(No miracles) MANUSCRIPT F (Oxford)	1499
1500	WYNKYN DE WORDE	1516
1600		
1700	ACTA SANCTORUM	1698
1800		
	PATROLOGIAE CURSUS COMPLETUS	1854
	PREFACE TO RAMSEY CHRONICLE	1886
1900	HORSTMAN	1901

KEY

⬭ — Manuscripts known or assumed to have existed

▭ — Printed editions

Manuscripts and editions <u>underlined</u> are extant.   See text for details.

incorporating some miracles which Goscelin had left out, or did not know. Alternatively, both this and D may have a common source (Goscelin himself?) which the one has rearranged and from which the other has selected (T being copied from D). Either theory is plausible and neither provable. Because B has further additions and was written at Ramsey it is easy to believe that the recording monks could not leave well alone: that in D we have Goscelin's story and the rest was their elaboration. The exotic origins certainly seem to be superimposed rather than an integral part of the story.

B and C, having apparently closed the account of St Ivo, immediately open up again with the translation of St Ivo's companions in Henry I's reign, and the stories follow: girl bewitched; spherical cripple; Pagan Peverel; woman and snake; Buckden gardener; woman of Dover; knight; undeserving monk. As explained in Chapter 8, these seem to be stories written up soon after they happened.

Both manuscripts end with the undeserving monk still in doubt, but at different points in the story. B ends abruptly with the monk's plea:

> "Now therefore, dearest friend of God, conceal our sins just a very little; pour out for us grateful prayers to Christ, so that having received favour, which we do not deserve, through you, we may praise the great works of God the Three-in-One, and glorify your name through Him for ever."

The last word is halfway down the left-hand column of a page and the writer continues directly with the heading for the *Life of St Margaret*, evidently unaware that the monk has not yet been cured. I can only suggest that the closing words of the monk's prayer (above) are so similar to the type of pious ending miracles often had that the scribe did not realise that there was more to come. By an unfortunate irony we are unable to use C to confirm or refute this idea, for St Ivo's is the last *Life* in the volume and at least one leaf is missing at the end, so that it finishes even more abruptly halfway through a word some four and a half sentences earlier. If C had more of the story than B it would have shown that it was not copied from B but that they had a common source. This is not improbable since the date as well as the uniformity of script in B shows it to be a 'fair copy' of the on-the-spot records.

Another pair of manuscripts exists for the third stage of the legend's development. This is the version written by John of Tynemouth in the earlier part of the fourteenth century. The earlier and more authoritative manuscript is another of the *Cotton Tiberius MSS, Ei*, and is also badly damaged by fire. (It could be deciphered with perseverance under ultra-violet light, but the daily limit of 2×10 minutes is prohibitive!) This manuscript (E) is the only one which preserves John of Tynemouth's arrangement by calendar order. It was written at St Albans and quite probably under the author's direct supervision. He was a monk at St Albans and he died, it is thought, of the Black Death in 1349, the same year that this volume was presented to Redborne, a priory cell nearby.

The same text is to be found in (F) another Oxford manuscript, *Tanner 15*, which was copied in 1499 by J Neell. Neell, however, uses alphabetical order. This rearrangement is thought to have been the work of John Capgrave who for a very long time received the entire credit for the massive work of compilation which John of Tynemouth had actually carried out. (Capgrave's manuscript was part of the Cotton collection which perished in the fire — *Otho xi*.) The contents of John of Tynemouth's *Life* are given in Chapter 10. It is clearly abridged from the 'Goscelin plus' version which he may have seen at Ramsey or Crowland, or which may have been in the library at St Albans itself: the link through Christina of Markyate has been explained. (The only extant biography of her is appended to *Cotton Tiberius Ei*.)

Lastly, of the manuscripts, a curious fragment, badly charred and previously unnoticed, is attached to the *Life of St Ivo* in *Cotton Tiberius Diii (f249)*. It is in a later hand (?fourteenth century) and occupies both sides of a single page. Many words and several whole lines are illegible, but it runs as follows. It starts with a paraphrase (not a copy) of St Ivo's parentage and his travels. Ivo settles in Slepe and lies in obscurity for four hundred years. The ploughman and his greedy companions are there and the bailiff Elnoth. Ivo appears to the smith in a dream and tells him to dig for the companions, and to tell the bailiff to inform abbot Eadnoth. The bailiff duly scoffs and is punished with the boots. The date (1001) is there. When the abbot translates the relics there are some lines — all but unreadable — evidently referring to the relics of the Kentish brothers, to the archbishop of Canterbury, to King Ethelred and the death of his brother St Edward. The one miracle which is reproduced in a summary form is Oswy of Ramsey, who neglected to sing the psalms. This single page does not match any of the manuscripts but is clearly a different abridgement of the version in B, and quite independent of John of Tynemouth's.

It was John's version, however, which kept Ivo from total obscurity. He included just about every known British saint in his book. In Capgrave's rearrangement it was one of the earliest books to be printed in England, by Wynkyn de Worde in 1516. The collection was widely drawn upon by Tudor and Stuart antiquarians and religious writers, including Nicholas Harpsfield who wrote in the mid-sixteenth century, but whose *English Church History* was not published until 1622. He seems to have been responsible for a false but charming piece of etymology:

> (Ivo) came to a certain place which was called Sleepe in English, which is in Latin *'dormitio'* . . . and that place became so famous that its old name was forgotten and the town was called Ives from that time. What wonderful foresight of God! The old name of the place seems to have known with a marvellous foreshadowing the sleep of blessed Ivo.

The John of Tynemouth version of St Ivo is the best served by editors. It was the first to be printed in 1516 as *'NOVA LEGENDA ANGLIE as collected by John of Tynemouth, John Capgrave, and others, and first printed, with New Lives, by Wynkyn de Worde a.d.mdxvi'*. This edition was carefully collated with the extant manuscripts by C Horstman and a new edition came out in 1901. As far as Ivo is concerned it represents reliably the two manuscripts, E and F.

The Goscelin version of the Life was partly published by the Bollandists in their *Acta Sanctorum, June II*, in 1698. This edition has the Prologue, the life and travels, the discovery and translation to Ramsey, and the building of the church at Slepe. No miracles are included at this point. The translation of Ivo's companions in the reign of Henry I is printed. An appendix of miracles, from Capgrave, is added, starting with the Venetian youth freed from his chains. This edition was used by J P Migne for his *Patrologiae Cursus Completus*, vol 155, published 1854. The preface which is printed in both editions makes it clear that the editor was not working from any of the manuscripts described above, for it says (in Latin):

> John Capgrave published another Life in *Legenda Sanctorum Anglie*, from which we give in an appendix some miracles worked by St Ivo's intercession, which, or at least some of them, Goscelin seems to have added, but the writer of our copy has missed out.

This means a copy with the twelfth century translation of St Ivo's companions but without any miracles.

The miracles waited until 1886 to be edited. W D Macray supplied the deficiency as an appendix to his preface to the *Ramsey Chronicle* in the Rolls Series. He used B and printed the whole text from where *Acta Sanctorum* left off, beginning with the leprous woman. There are a few slips, eg in the story of Alwold of Stanton Macray begins *Nec* for Hec and later has *vivam* (live) instead of *niveam* (snow-white) to describe the hen, but generally there is nothing more serious than this.

Thus the whole body of mediaeval writings about St Ivo may be found in print in the original Latin except for the added first chapter relating his origins in Persia *'In civitate Frianeos'* which John of Tynemouth only excerpted. As this is the most purely fantastic and historically the least useful, perhaps it matters less.

APPENDIX TWO
Notes and Sources

Immersion in the cult of St Ivo has involved much reading. Below I cite authorities for readers who wish to follow my deductions and arguments.

General
The following have been indispensable reference books:
F BARLOW, *The English Church 1000-1066*, 2nd ed. London 1979.
F BARLOW, *The English Church 1066-1154*, London 1979.
D KNOWLES and R N HADCOCK, *Medieval Religious Houses*, London 1971.
D KNOWLES, *The Monastic Order in England*, 2nd ed. Cambridge 1966.
F M STENTON, *Anglo-Saxon England*, 2nd ed. Oxford 1947.

Chapter 1
An impression of pre-Conquest fenland derives from H C DARBY, *The Changing Fenland*, Cambridge 1983; *Victoria County History — Huntingdonshire*, London 1932.

The two quotations about the fens are from FELIX, Life of Guthlac (my translation): the most recent edition is by B COLGRAVE, Cambridge 1956. Daniel DEFOE's *Tour thro' the whole island of Great Britain* was first published in 1724-7 and may be read in an edition by G D H COLE and D C BROWNING, 2 vols., London 1962.

The history of Ramsey Abbey can be read in its two collections of documents: *Chronicon Abbatiae Rameseiensis*, ed W D MACRAY, London 1886 and *Cartularium Monasterii de Rameseia*, ed in 3 vols. W H HART and P A LYONS, London 1884-93. Supplementary information and commentary on the endowments are in C R HART, *The Early Charters of Eastern England*, Leicester 1966. A special study of Ramsey's acquisitions from the family of Aethelstan Mannessone is by C R HART: 'Eadnoth, First Abbot of Ramsey, and the Foundation of Chatteris and St Ives' in *Proceedings of the Cambridge Antiquarian Society* 56-57 (1964), pp 61-7.

The cult of relics is fully explored in P J GEARY, *Furta Sacra: Thefts of Relics in the Central Middle Ages*, Princeton 1978. The long quotation about the discovery of St Ivo's bones and all subsequent quotations, unless other attribution is given, is from my translation of the *Life and Miracles of St Ivo*.

Chapter 2
For Ivo's Persia, the following may be consulted:
J P ASMUSSEN, 'Christians in Iran' in *The Cambridge History of Iran* vol 3 ii, Cambridge 1983, pp 924-48.
J LABOURT, *Le Christianisme dans l'empire perse sous la dynastie sassanide*, Paris 1904.

The suggestion regarding the inscription was made by D E E USHER in *The Mediaeval Fair of St Ives*, Cambridge 1953.

The most complete history of St Neots is by G C GORHAM, *History and Antiquities of Eynesbury and St Neots*, London 1820. The Anglo-Saxon Royal Saints are the subject of a forthcoming book by S Ridyard, Cambridge.

Theories regarding the origins of St Ivo's cult are set out in G H DOBLE, 'St Ivo, Bishop and Confessor, Patron of the Town of St Ives' in *Laudate* 12 (1934), pp 149-56, and in the *Dictionary of Christian Biography* under St Ivo in vol 3, London 1882.

Chapter 3
For Eadnoth the best account is HART 'Eadnoth' (see Chapter 1). M L Clarke of Cholsey, Oxon. sent me an informative note on Germanus and the Chronicle of John of Wallingford.

I am grateful to Ottar Osaland of Bergen for help with Siward. The most useful book is C J A OPPERMANN, *The English Missionaries in Sweden and Finland*, London 1937. *Domesday Book — Huntingdonshire* has been edited by J MORRIS, Chichester 1975.

The best modern account of Herbert Losinga is by J W ALEXANDER 'Herbert of Norwich 1091-1119' in *Studies in Medieval and Renaissance History* 6 (1969), pp 119-232.

Chapter 4

Goscelin is the subject of an unpublished PhD thesis (Virginia 1973) by T J HAMILTON, *Goscelin of Canterbury: a critical study of his life, works and accomplishments*. This is not only excessively long (1024pp) but contains errors of detail (eg Selsey for Cholsey, and an argument based on the sum $1001 - 600 = 5$ centuries, which brings Ivo to England 'almost a century' before its conversion!) and some disputable interpretations. In particular Hamilton believes the cult of St Ivo to have been popular in the eleventh century and Ramsey 'a famous pilgrimage center'. My own views should be clear above. A more accessible account of Goscelin's career is in F BARLOW (ed.), *Life of King Edward*, London 1962. A very interesting comparison for St Ivo, since it deals with another of Goscelin's *Lives* is D W ROLLASON, *The Mildrith Legend: a Study in Early Medieval Hagiography in England*, Leicester 1982.

There is an extensive literature on miracles and pilgrimages, of which the following are representative:

R FINUCANE, *Miracles and Pilgrims: Popular Beliefs in Medieval England*, London 1977.

C G LOOMIS, *White Magic*, Cambridge, Mass. 1948.

J SUMPTION, *Pilgrimage*, London 1974.

J C R Riley-Smith has a note on eleventh century celestial phenomena in his forthcoming book on the First Crusade.

Chapter 5

I am grateful to Dr P M Morris of Buckden who read an early draft of my translation and commented on various ailments inflicted or alleviated by Ivo.

Chapter 6

Two fascinating accounts of early mediaeval medicine are recommended:

W BONSER, *The Medical Background of Anglo-Saxon England*, London 1963.

S RUBIN, *Medieval English Medicine*, Newton Abbot 1974.

Chapter 7

See HART, *Early Charters* (see Chapter 1) for Godric's will.

Chapter 8

The story of Pagan Peverel has inspired me to more detailed research which may be found in P W EDBURY (ed.), *Crusade and Settlement*, Cardiff 1985.

Chapter 9

The following are the editions used for mediaeval writers. Except for Florence, the translations are mine.

FLORENCE OF WORCESTER, *Chronicon ex Chronicis*, ed. and tr. T FORESTER, London 1854.

WILLIAM OF MALMESBURY, *Gesta Pontificum Anglorum*, ed. Nesa HAMILTON, London 1870.

HENRY OF HUNTINGDON, *History of the English*, ed. T ARNOLD, London 1879.

Liber Eliensis, ed. E O BLAKE, London 1962.

Chronicon Abbatiae Rameseiensis, ed. W D MACRAY, London 1886.

Cartularium Monasterii de Rameseia, 3 vols ed. W H HART and P A LYONS, London 1884-93.

JOHN OF BROMPTON in *Decem Scriptores*, ed. R TWYSDEN, London 1652.

JOHN OF WALLINGFORD, *The Chronicle attributed to...*, ed. R VAUGHAN, London 1958.

MATTHEW PARIS, *Chronica Maiora*, ed. F MADDEN, London 1866-9.

F WORMALD (ed.), *English Benedictine Kalendars before 1100*, London 1933.

F WORMALD (ed.), *English Benedictine Kalendars after AD 1100*, 2 vols., London 1939, 1946.

Relic lists are from an unpublished PhD thesis (London 1975) by I G THOMAS.

See C H TALBOT (ed. and tr.), *The Life of Christina of Markyate*, Oxford 1959, for the St Albans connection.

Chapter 10

The mediaeval fair at St Ives is described in:

W ADDISON, *English Fairs and Markets*, London 1953.

D E E USHER, *The Mediaeval Fair of St Ives*, Cambridge 1953.

E WEDERMEYER, 'Social Groupings at the Fair of St Ives (1275-1302)' in *Mediaeval Studies* 32 (1970) pp 27-59.

Details of editions of JOHN OF TYNEMOUTH may be found in Appendix 1. For a picture of late mediaeval England see J J JUSSERAND, *English Wayfaring Life in the Middle Ages (XIVth century)*, 2nd ed. London 1889.

Margaret Hunt's conviction for witchcraft was found in W H HALE, *A series of precedents. . . ,* London 1847 (reference in K THOMAS, *Religion and the Decline of Magic,* London 1971).

F ARNOLD-FOSTER, *Studies in Church Dedications,* London 1899, was the starting point for research into the other St Ives. Application to the parishes concerned brought charming replies but little new information. I thank Mrs B N Furse and Mr J S Wenmouth of St Ive in Cornwall and Mrs A Tuck of Leadgate in County Durham for their courtesy.

The frivolous conclusion quotes from W C SELLAR and R J YEATMAN, *1066 And All That,* London 1930.

Appendix One
Full details of editions are given in the appendix.
N HARPSFIELD, *Historia Anglicana Ecclesiastica. . . ,* was ed. R GIBBON, Douai 1622.
An important review of Doble's account of Ivo (see Chapter 2) is to be found in *Analecta Bollandiana* 54 (1936) pp 203-4. By P GROSJEAN, it refers to earlier notes in the *Analecta* and to the *Bibliotheca Hagiographica Latina Antiquae et Mediae Aetatis,* vol 1 p 685 nos 4621-4, Brussels 1898-9, which help to unravel the textual history of the *Life and Miracles of St Ivo.*

It is possible you have reached the end of this book without knowing where I stand on the truth of St Ivo's miracles. I should like to end with the finest quotation of all, from section 28 of Sir Thomas Browne's *Religio Medici* of 1643:

Therefore, that miracles have been, I do believe; that they may yet be wrought by the living, I do not deny: but have no confidence in those which are fathered on the dead. And this hath ever made me suspect the efficacy of relics, to examine the bones, question the habits and appertenances of saints...